9/27/02
$ 11.00

making sense of

strategy

making sense of
strategy

TONY MANNING

AMACOM
American Management Association

New York • Atlanta • Brussels • Buenos Aires • Chicago • London • Mexico City
San Francisco • Shanghai • Tokyo • Toronto • Washington, D. C.

Special discounts on bulk quantities of AMACOM books are available to corporations, professional associations, and other organizations. For details, contact Special Sales Department, AMACOM, a division of American Management Association, 1601 Broadway, New York, NY 10019. Tel.: 212-903-8316. Fax: 212-903-8083.
Web site: www.amacombooks. org

This publication is designed to provide accurate and authoritative information in regard to the subject matter covered. It is sold with the understanding that the publisher is not engaged in rendering legal, accounting, or other professional service. If legal advice or other expert assistance is required, the services of a competent professional person should be sought.

Cataloging-in-Publication data has been applied for and is on record at the Library of Congress.

Publication © Zebra 2001
Text © Tony Manning 2001
All rights reserved.
Printed in the United States of America.

First published in 2001 by Zebra, an imprint of Struik Publishers, PO Box 1144, Cape Town 8000, South Africa. AMACOM edition published in 2002 by arrangement with Struik Publishers.

Printing number

10 9 8 7 6 5 4 3 2 1

PRINCIPLES

1. If you don't make a difference, you don't matter.
2. You can't make a difference to everyone.
3. Strategy must enable your organization to make a difference that matters to a critical mass of the "right" customers.
4. Strategy connects the purpose and values of your organization with those of its customers and other external stakeholders.
5. It may be easy to clone a product, but it's impossible to clone a community. So a vital goal of strategy is to create and sustain a unique community.
6. Purpose and values hold a community together, drive teams to seek their potential, and provide the context in which individuals will volunteer their imagination and spirit.
7. Shared ideas lead to shared meaning. The more openly and honestly ideas are shared, the greater the level of trust will be, the more efforts will be aligned – and the more ideas will emerge.
8. People value work that makes them feel valued. When *they* make strategy, they matter. And *they* own the results, so effective execution is more likely.
9. Strategic management is *conversation*. It informs, focuses attention and effort, triggers fresh insights, lights up the imagination, energizes people, and inspires performance.
10. Strategic conversation provides a context for personal and group learning. Your message must be compelling, simple, clear, and believable, or you won't sell it. It must also be complex and challenging, or no one will buy it. And it must be repeated with relentless consistency.

CONTENTS

For Lee.
A magical person
whose caring and courage and wisdom
make the difference that matters.

making sense of
strategy

INTRODUCTION

INTRODUCTION

L et's cut the b.s. and cut straight to the chase. Strategy is not rocket science. It's about listening to customers, asking some pretty simple questions, making some choices, and getting people to support your decisions.

Strategy is the ultimate responsibility of every business leader. Companies succeed when they get it right and fail when they get it wrong. The fact that more companies fail than succeed says that something is very wrong indeed with the state of strategy. It's also an indictment of leadership.

This new century is a time of extraordinary complexity, opportunity, and risk. Business is a 24/7 activity. Markets are global, competitors are increasingly hostile, and change occurs faster than at any other time in history. Managing almost any organization gets harder by the minute. There's too much to do and too many new challenges. Things need more thought, but there's less time to turn ideas into action.

Smart people have been writing about management for close to 100 years, and they've offered "solutions" to just about every business problem. Yet executives everywhere still seek The Answer to a simple question:

How do you choose what to do . . . and how do you get it done?

Or, to put it differently, what is the best way to take your company from here to the future and make a bundle of money on the way?

Whether you think of your company as "old economy" or "new economy," as "bricks-and-mortar," "B2B" (business-to-business), "B2C" (business-to-consumer), or whatever, the race for tomorrow's customers and profits hinges on two things: *business model design* and *implementation capability*. So best you wrap your mind around what really matters and get busy with it fast.

Best, too, that you sort through your toolkit and quickly toss out some of the junk that's taking up your time and attention. Like most executives, you probably have stuff in there that weighs you down and stops you getting your job done. Like most organizations, yours is probably jammed with meetings, buzzwords, workshops, projects, studies, and reports that add precisely zero to your bottom line.

Ironically, one trigger for trouble is the management know-how industry, which in recent years has caught fire. It preaches innovation, yet is a major cause of *organizational logjams*.

Every discipline—art, medicine, mathematics, or whatever—evolves over time. Now and then a quantum shift occurs that changes the game: cubism, penicillin, Einstein's theory of relativity. But management thinking barely moves. Concepts are recycled, repackaged, and pumped back onto the market as brilliant breakthroughs, as the ultimate success formula, as the definitive solution. At the very time that we're warned over and over that more of the same is the kiss of corporate death, in reality it's the order of the day. And those who warn about it most are often its most ardent advocates.

Managers try hard to create the impression that they're sensible, logical, and practical. Yet they're suckers for snake oil.

Business school academics churn out articles that often become books and are then leveraged into audio and videotapes, CDs, and seminars and lucrative speaking assignments in exotic places. Management consultants boast about "thought leadership" and promise to bring "best practices" to their clients' businesses. But you don't have to be an expert to make hay in the field of management ideas.

Yachtsmen, football coaches, and orchestra conductors make fortunes sharing their experience with people trying to make a buck from auto assembly, microchip fabrication, or commercializing software code. If you've crossed the Sahara on a motorbike, climbed Mount Everest (or maybe even a lesser mountain like Annapurna or Kilimanjaro), or spent a year with a mystic in Nepal, you're in business.

Books for managers fly faster and in greater numbers onto the shelves. Some have serious titles and clunky prose that ensure that most readers won't get past Chapter 1. Others are catchier and jammed with bullet points and checklists.

Many best-sellers of the past two decades have been written as if for idiots. Parables are popular, and "Bill" and "Mary" feature in lots of them, along with mentors like "The Executive." The heroes of one winner are "little people" and a couple of mice. And there are any number of titles promising the wisdom of dolphins or foxes or wolves; the inspiration of eagles; lessons from some ancient Japanese warrior, Bushmen hunters, the Marines, or a trendy Californian chef; or insights from survivors of aircraft crashes, cancer, or a cocaine habit.

Most of the people I talk to complain that busy-ness is killing them. They have too much to do, and too little time. Since this is the Information Age, they naturally all suffer from information overload. Yet most management books are designed to add to their woes. They're dense with case studies, anecdotes, and quotes from famous executives. And who has time any more to plow through 300 or 400 pages of turgid theory?

This book is the antidote.

It may be the last business book you'll ever need to read. It certainly should be the *first*. For it tells you everything you need to know about strategic management, yet you can read it in less than an hour. (So that leaves you the rest of your life to actually get things done!)

Making Sense of Strategy is based on the latest management thinking, as well as my own experience of what actually goes on in companies and what really works. It captures views that have developed over the past century, from writers listed in the bibliography and from many others, too. Some of the ideas have appeared in my earlier books, and I use them here because they have been extensively "field-tested" over a long period.

Unlike other books, which tend to focus on one aspect of management or another, this one presents a holistic view. It gives you an original—and effective—way of making the difference that matters. In addition to its back-to-basics approach, it's unique for seven reasons:

1. It makes strategic planning a sensible and powerful business tool at a time when many people say that planning is a relic of the past and a waste of time in a chaotic, fast-changing world.
2. It builds on a wide range of business concepts, including value chains and value constellations, core competence, activity systems, co-opetition, and hypercompetition to give you a thoroughly *practical* way of thinking about your strategy.
3. It weaves ideas from many fields—strategy, systems theory, chaos and complexity, human resources management, change management, total quality management, lean thinking, leadership, and others—into an integrated and understandable process.
4. It helps you focus on what really matters, thus avoiding the dreaded corporate disease of "interventionitis" (which paralyzes people by overwhelming them with initiatives and projects—customer service today, quality tomorrow; a dash of cost cutting; a stab at team building; a dose of reengineering; or a sudden infatuation with e-commerce).
5. It provides a step-by-step approach to creating, implementing, and evaluating strategy. You can also use the tools in any combination that meets your needs.
6. The emphasis is on *growth through action*—on getting results fast, on learning by doing, and on making strategy and change simultaneous activities.
7. You can actually *do* something with it!

Like politics, business is the art of the possible. *Making Sense of Strategy* will help you make things possible. Whether you're a practicing executive, a student or teacher of management, an investor, an investment analyst, or a business journalist, this book will help you make a difference.

There are many questions in the pages that follow. You can use them to diagnose the current health of your organization by thinking about them in the present tense. Or you can use them to create tomorrow's strategy by considering what might be. Both approaches are worthwhile. And remember—*the first answer is seldom the only one or the best one*. So keep digging. The more you ask, the more likely you are to get past the superficial stuff and hit gold!

TONY MANNING

P.S. In the spirit of good conversation, please let me know what you think of *Making Sense of Strategy*. You can e-mail me at strategist@tonymanning.com. My website—www.tonymanning.com—has lots of other information you may find helpful.

1
CONTEXT

T he purpose of a leader is to create a context in which people will perform to their potential. This "mental space" is where they discover and test themselves and where they reveal (or conceal) their magic. Context is a product of conversation.

Organizations, then, are *managed conversations*. People inside them talk to one another all day long about what they must do and how they do it. They also talk to a variety of outsiders—customers, suppliers, government, and so on. If the right people are involved and if these conversations are open, honest, constructive, and positive, good things happen. But if key people are left out, and if the conversation is blocked, devious, destructive, or negative, trouble is ensured. "Nourishing conversation" is vital to success. "Toxic conversation" guarantees failure.

In shaping their context, strategists must do three things:

1. **Make choices**. You have to decide which customers and markets to chase, what products or services to offer, and how to apply your resources.
2. **Win "votes."** You have to exist in harmony with many stakeholders, and you have to persuade some of them (especially your people, your suppliers, and your customers) to *volunteer* their imagination and spirit to your cause.
3. **Build capacity**. You have to develop your organization's "strategic IQ" so that your people can think and act appropriately as you head into a surprising future.

The 228 words you've just read tell you why some companies win and others lose. They explain why so many change efforts fail to deliver the expected results and why companies struggle to survive and grow. And they highlight what leaders must do to make a difference.

Choices, commitment, and capacity are not the products of machines. All result from people talking to one another. All come from that everyday activity—*conversation*—that we mostly take for granted and often use carelessly because it's such an integral part of our lives.

Much of our daily conversation is a *default* activity: it just sort of happens. By contrast, "strategic conversation" is no accident. It's a *deliberate* process and the No. 1 leadership tool. All else rests on it. So you need to think about it systematically, craft it carefully, and use it purposefully.

The first task of a leader is to provide a clear point of view—"There's the hill we're aiming at . . . these are the results we want . . . this is how we should conduct ourselves . . . here are our priorities . . . this is what we'll do to get where we want to go." This is the context in which people work.

The ongoing task is to focus and inspire them. We all know that "what gets measured gets managed." But we conveniently forget that it's only what is *spoken* about—constantly, passionately, consistently—that will be either measured or managed. Talk about the right *issues* in the right *way* to the right *people*, and extraordinary things happen; but get the conversation wrong, and you're sunk.

When a leader speaks constantly about customer service, that's what people pay attention to. If he or she speaks fanatically about costs—or productivity, teamwork, innovation, or whatever—then those are the things that count.

Just as language influences the way a society works, so does it impact on the behavior—and the bottom line—of a company. But when did you last hear managers say, "Let's talk about what we need to talk about" or, "Let's think about the words we use around here"? Probably never. After all, they have better, cleverer things to do. (And maybe there's a communications manager who handles communication!)

Management tools come and go with mostly disappointing results because the strategic conversation that should be their base is missing or ineffective. Executives work on "superstructure," when their foundations are weak. They call on sophisticated concepts when the basics are not in place.

If you were to ask almost any top executive to list their three most critical concerns, you'd probably hear: strategy, leadership, and change management. If you then looked for answers to these issues, you'd find little common ground among them. They're treated as three distinct challenges. Yet they interlock and overlap so tightly it's virtually impossible to deal with them separately and still be effective.

The language problem in business begins when you ask people what they understand by strategy. Here are some common answers:

"It's a plan for taking your company into the future."
"Vision, mission, values, and action plans."
"A long-term view of where you're headed."
"A SWOT analysis."*
"The analysis you do to make sure you hit the numbers."

Now ask whose responsibility it is, and the answer is almost always the same: "Top management!"

Strategy, it seems, is something that a few smart and powerful people think about. Then they pass their wisdom down the line in the form of instructions, and the drones get busy.

Or that's the theory.

In real life, the folks at the top might indeed think about "the big issues." They might agree on "big, hairy, audacious goals." And they might produce terrific documents and slide shows and make stirring speeches. But then something goes wrong.

Things change in the world around them. There's a surprise a minute—and not all of them pleasant. Their people don't do what they're told. Their great plans produce mediocre results. Even if by some miracle they manage to do what they intended, it turns out to be wrong.

---

* Strengths, weaknesses, opportunities, threats, an exercise that forms part of just about every planning workshop and fills lots of flipchart pages, yet seldom leads to radical thinking. More often, the same issues get recycled year after year and never go away.

Most companies have a shorter life than most people. For all the time, energy, and money that goes into making them survive and thrive, the results are disappointing. Reengineering cuts costs . . . but kills employee loyalty. Customer service improves . . . but customers think it's worse. You spend fortunes on change and improvement . . . but three out of four change efforts don't work as they should. You think you'll put your company on steroids with a new strategy . . . and the damned thing shrivels up and dies on you!

WHAT'S GOING ON?

John Lennon put it perfectly when he said, "Life is what happens when you're busy making other plans."

Life doesn't wait for your market analysis, your consultant's advice, or your 500-page plan. Nor does it stop while you rethink, reengineer, or reorganize. It's a dynamic, complex, surprising, exhilarating, wonderful—and sometimes shocking—process that sweeps you along . . . or sweeps you away.

This gives you a simple choice: either you deal with things as they *are*, or you close your eyes to reality and plan for things as you'd *like them to be*.

If you think that's a no-brainer, ask yourself why so many companies get into trouble so quickly, and so few enjoy a long and happy life. It can't be because most executives are dimwits. It has to be that:

- They have their heads in the clouds, from where they happily ignore what's going on around them.
- They interpret environmental signals to suit their own mental models, rather than looking the facts and the future right in the eye and doing what they must to adapt and survive.
- They fail to build the internal organizational capabilities that fit changing external realities, so though they may be successful for a time, their performance sooner or later slumps.
- They can't get things done.

In theory, corporate evolution is a tidy matter that's taken care of by top management. In practice, it's a messy process. A lot of it happens way out at the edges, far from the planners, the scenarios, and the spreadsheets, where "low-level people" serve customers, make stuff, fix things, punch buttons, sign documents, interpret events, and otherwise do their own thing.

People at the top don't have "line of sight" to the real world. The rest don't have "line of sight" to the reasoning behind their organization's strategy. This blindness makes both groups less effective than they might be.

The bosses think they're firmly in charge. In fact, they're bounced around by issues and events. Hard as they try to shape strategy, it's to a great extent shaped for them. While they imagine themselves as being all-powerful, the world around them goes on with its business—and molds the context for their business decisions and actions.

Two of the hottest business themes in recent years have been core competence and chaos theory. Volumes have been written about both, and they're favorites on the conference scene. Yet all you need to know is this:

- *You have to be exceptionally good at something.* You have to build strengths today for tomorrow. And since all capabilities hinge on the "mind of your organization," it's your most valuable asset and your best weapon. The ability to anticipate, imagine, and innovate is the most critical competence of all. The more widely spread this competence, the better. And the best way—possibly even the *only* way—to develop and leverage it is through strategic conversation.

- *You don't have to know everything.* The world is inherently unpredictable. Control freaks get hurt. You cannot get to the future in a straight line. But you *can* take advantage of surprises by involving your people in a rich, robust strategic conversation that makes every one of them the eyes, ears, and brain of your organization. When you're all alert and learning, when you're sharing and testing ideas, and pushing and inspiring one another, chaos becomes fuel for growth. Serendipity becomes a spark for change. Surprises energize you.

Perhaps the most difficult thing for any leader to accept is the tension between freedom and control. Disregarded, it causes awful problems. Embraced, it brings remarkable results.

Strategy demands discipline. Leaders need to be firm and clear about what they expect. But beware of strangling your organization. The context you create will imprison or liberate people. It'll either give them courage and confidence and build their competence, or it will convince them that ordinary is OK. It'll either empower them to do roughly the best thing most of the time, or it will ensure that they underperform constantly and screw up regularly. (Which means that you have to keep them on a short leash and waste your own time mopping up behind them.)

REMEMBER LIFE CYCLES?

By now, every executive knows about life cycles. Yet for some reason, most forget about them or pretend they apply only to someone else. But they affect all of us, and we ignore them at our peril.

Every living thing goes through a fairly predictable process of birth, growth, maturity, decline, and death. Nothing is forever. Companies are no exception. But whereas other organisms—people, animals, plants—age and die no matter how well they adapt to their external environment, the lifetime of organizations can be extended. Those that adapt best will outperform and outlive their competitors.

Companies are born into a changing world, and it keeps changing. The conditions that exist when an entrepreneur hangs out his or her shingle don't last for long. So the challenge is to extend the time between a company's first breath and its last gasp (Figure 1-1).

The only way to do this is to continually reinvent your organization so that it "fits" the emerging conditions around it, to create new "S-curves" that keep your sales and profits on an upward path, defying the gravitational pull of "more of the same" (Figure 1-2).

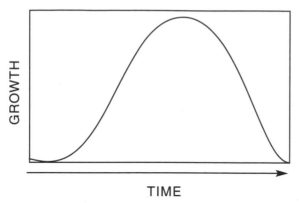

FIGURE 1-1 *Every living thing goes through a fairly predictable life cycle. Most companies die shortly after birth. On average, those that survive will last about 30 years. A few last well over 100 years.*

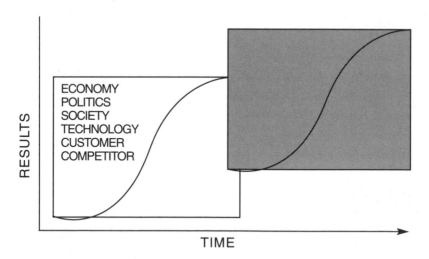

FIGURE 1-2 *Organizations can rejuvenate themselves through improvement and innovation—by doing the same things better and by doing different things. But they must at all times live in harmony with the world around them.*

BEATING THE ODDS

Business is always a gamble. It involves a lot of guesswork. There are few certainties and many possibilities.

While there's plenty of information about most things today, the future is a mystery. No one knows what's going to happen an hour from now, let alone in six months or ten years. The best you can do is make some assumptions *based on what is already going on.*

Beware, however, of then assuming that events will unfold in a straight line to the future. Current trends may signal future ones but do not guarantee them. So although you may gather reams of documents, listen to dozens of experts, or commission tons of research, you sooner or later have to do what *feels* right. Put bluntly, you have to go with your gut.

Some people seem to have an inborn ability to make the right calls (or they're just luckier than most). Experience does hone judgment (though it may just stop you taking a lot of chances that might have paid off). But the fact is, we all wind up guessing.

In the real world, success in most fields involves a lot of bumbling. You might say that we fall (and fail) our way into the future. So picking yourself up fast—recovering, learning, and moving on—is the real gift. Action is a surer way to the future than endless analysis. Surviving to fight another day is smarter than committing suicide with a single stroke.

Yesterday's strategic planners dreamed about big S-curves with five- or ten-year horizons. In some industries this still makes sense, because you have to invest hefty sums and the payoff is way off. Besides, laying big bets may bring big wins—in fact, may be the only way to the jackpot. And macho leaders are admired for their boldness—which may inspire valuable confidence. So obviously you should have a long-term view of where you want to go. And obviously you should aim for the single S-curve that will ensure leadership. But be aware that one "visionary" move can sink you.

For most companies, the way to win is by trying more things faster—by "hustling with a purpose" (Figure 1-3). By laying lots of small bets, you can afford the losses and learn from the wins. And, with luck, the incremental changes you make will add up to a meaningful difference.

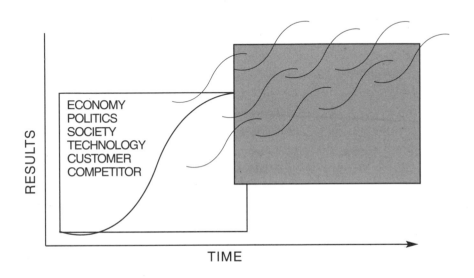

FIGURE 1-3 Laying *one big bet on a future you can't quite see is dangerous practice. It's much safer—and smarter—to lay lots of small bets and to "experiment your way into the future." This way, you can apply new insights and ideas as you go, so you get the most from each new move.*

Many companies treat strategic planning as an annual ritual, a calendar-driven activity tied to the budget cycle. Some do it even less often and less regularly. Between stabs, life goes on, and issues that screamed for attention yesterday are forgotten by the next planning meeting. Today's boldest, bravest intentions take so long to turn into action that people laugh them off and keep busy with stuff that really matters. But worst of all, this stop-start, quantum-leap approach ensures that you wind up having to change too much, too fast, and usually when it doesn't suit you. When you defy reality, you make nonsense of strategy.

Although it might make sense to get your team together from time to time to review where you've been or to brainstorm new possibilities, strategic management is an ongoing process. It needs daily attention. If you're not engaged in a *constant* conversation about what lies ahead, what it means, and what you should do about it, the world will pass you by. (You might find that radical change isn't necessary; constant improvement could be just what's needed to preserve your competitive edge for ages.)

This brings us to a question—or an argument—that bedevils organizations: should you talk *strategy* or *tactics*? But does it matter? Who cares what label you apply, as long as you do the sensible thing!

TWO SCHOOLS OF THOUGHT

For all that's written and said about strategy, it remains a fuzzy activity. Part of the reason for this is that it embraces everything a company does. Part of the reason is that the gurus don't agree on the best way to approach it.

However, when you cut through all the pet theories and buzzwords, you come to the fact that there are essentially two schools of thought about the subject:

1. **The outside-in school.** This lot believes that an organization is a "prisoner of its environment," and can do only what the world around it allows. The task of managers is to create the best possible fit between their organization's internal strengths and weaknesses and whatever external opportunities and threats there may be.

2. **The inside-out school.** To this group, the greatest constraint on a company's performance is its own mindset. With enough ambition—or "stretch"—and with the right core competencies, just about anything is possible. Aggressive, creative companies can take on all comers and conquer the world.

So which is right? Which is best?

The answer, of course, is both.

The environment in which you compete does influence what you can and cannot do. It may help, hinder, or hurt you. But its effect is determined to a great extent *by the way you choose to deal with it.*

Some industries seem to be inherently more profitable than others. But the profitability of companies *within* any industry varies widely and there are winners and losers in all of them. So companies obviously differ in the way they respond to their circumstances.

Growth is possible in many seemingly hopeless industries. To be depressed that you're in a so-called sunset industry is as ridiculous as being overexcited because you're in a sunrise industry. Life is what you make it. The future is a matter of choice, not chance. You may face exceptional challenges, but it's how you think and act that matters.

Corporate growth is not a gift. Nor does it happen by accident—and certainly not in the long run. Luck helps, and it may be a huge factor in a company's success, but you can't rely on it. So best you create the circumstances in which things are mostly likely to go your way.

To be a leader in your particular domain, you need to know as much as possible about conditions outside your company's walls. You need to see not only the problems but, more especially, the opportunities. And to take advantage of them, you need the "right stuff"—not just *hard* assets like cash, factories, technology, systems, and tools but also *soft* assets like reputation, brands, and patents and, even more important, soft *human* assets such as attitude, imagination, knowledge, skills, and spirit.

Executives in poorly performing companies are quick to blame external factors for their plight. It's everyone's fault but their own; they are victim to forces or events around them. Their unspoken cry is, "In the face of these realities, I'm helpless!"

What nonsense! The fact is, you have a huge amount of influence over your own fortunes. No matter how you're performing today, and no matter what conditions prevail around you, you can probably change things dramatically. You can fix your company if it's sick. You can grow your sales and profits. You can improve your customer satisfaction rating. You can make your organization a better place to work, a better citizen, a better investment.

How? By getting the basics right. By having a "fingertip feel" for what's happening in your business arena, creating an appropriate value proposition and business model, applying the First Principles of Business Competition,* and executing effectively.

When you're not doing these things, your company will be undervalued. You'll think it's a dog, and so will others. So you might be suckered into carving it up, selling it, or even closing it; customers and suppliers will spook; investors will be jumpy or will take their money and run. The business media won't help either, because when they sniff trouble, they have a story.

My advice to companies that are in this dangerous spiral: *Slow down . . . and hurry up!* Slow down and take careful stock. Then hurry up and do something.

Do your homework. Get the facts. Look critically at what you're doing and why you're doing it that way. Question your assumptions. Put your "best practices" under a spotlight and work them over. Systematically develop a new strategy based on reality and focused on high-leverage issues. And drive aggressively forward. *Fast.*

You don't need a magic wand. You don't need miracles. You don't need a fairy godmother. What you do need is common sense, a toolkit of critical concepts, a way to put a rocket under your organization—and the leadership strength to do it.

Information + imagination + inspiration + action = results

Let's start the journey to growth by looking at some key concepts that underpin the work of strategists.

---

* The First Principles are discussed on page 26.

2
CONCEPTS

E xecutives face many challenges and have many responsibilities. But *growth tops the list*. They must grow sales, profits, and people. They must enhance their organizational capabilities. And they must rejuvenate their organizations and replenish their resources.

Some people would like to give growth a bad name, and many argue that there are more important things for business to worry about. But growth is necessary—and good—for several reasons:

1. *It makes an organization fit for the future.* All resources get used up, weaken, or become inappropriate over time. If you don't grow a new supply, you will neither survive nor be able to exploit new opportunities. And if there's one thing you can bet on, it's that competing tomorrow will be more, not less, costly and that if you don't immediately start developing the strengths you'll need, you may never afford them.

2. *It motivates and inspires employees.* People like to work for companies that are going places. They're turned on by success. Winning market share, expanding into new territory, gobbling up competitors, extending a plant, or broadening your product line are all challenging and exciting. What's more, tackling such tasks stretches people and gives them the opportunity to acquire new knowledge, develop new skills, and become more confident.

3. *It impresses customers.* Growth enhances your reputation and gives buyers confidence that (a) they're riding a winning horse and (b) you'll be around in the future. Their word-of-mouth recommendation is the most powerful promotional tool of all. Their support fuels a virtuous cycle of continuous progress.

4. *It satisfies investors.* There are many places investors can put their money, and growth and risk are key factors when they choose between opportunities.

Naturally, they want to get as much as possible back; they also want to know that their investment is reasonably secure. A growth record gives them confidence on both counts.

Growth is the ultimate measure of corporate success or failure. The most innovative business in the world would not be admired for long if it started losing customers, cutting back on research and development, or running up financial losses. That you fight to save the rainforests counts for little when your profits dive. Your stand against the exploitation of third world workers, your support for the arts, or your commitment to educate the children of your workers mean nothing if you don't produce the surpluses to pay for them, if they don't add to your bottom line, or if they don't make your company more valuable.

Growth keeps companies alive. Lack of it causes their death. The evidence so is clear-cut on this score that it's pointless asking, "Do we really need to grow?" or "Shouldn't we just grow slowly?" The real questions are, "What is our growth ambition?," "How *fast* should we grow?," and "How will we do it?"

Your growth trajectory will vary, depending on circumstances. Sometimes, it makes sense to "go for it" with a vengeance, to spend freely on market share through new product launches, price cuts, promotions, or distribution improvements or through acquisitions or alliances. At other times, you need to slow down, get your house in order, and wait for the next opportunity. Always, though, *your strategic conversation must focus on growth.*

Growth matters. Money talks. Strategy is a means to make growth happen, and to make more money than you use. Talk about growth and money should be central to your strategic conversation. When you put them there, you raise their profile, you emphasize their importance, and you focus your team's attention on the measures that important outsiders use.

SHAREHOLDERS FIRST

Companies have to satisfy many stakeholders, and the pressures are growing for them to be good citizens, to do good works, and to care for everything from their own people to spotted owls. But the interests of one stakeholder rank above all others. Companies must first satisfy their *shareholders*. They must first make money.

As we will see, you should obviously strive for win-win relationships with all your stakeholders. But you will be faced with tradeoffs. When that happens, remember that no business can be run as a social club (at least, not for long) and that the long-term survival of your organization is your first responsibility.

The fashionable notion that all stakeholders rank equally is not grounded in reality. Companies that balance the demands of shareholders, customers, and their own people tend to outperform others. But let's be clear: the reason to care for customers is that they're the source of *economic profit*—the indicator that investors care most about. The reason to care for employees is that they produce products and services and drive sales. Both groups, in other words, serve the investor.

When investors support a company, it can afford to compete for the future. When they head for hills, they take its lifeblood with them. Mostly, they tolerate ups and downs in the revenue and earnings cycles. But they expect the longterm trajectory to be strongly upward. And they know that growth is possible in good times or bad, and in just about every industry.

As is the case with all stakeholders, shareholders' views of a company are based partly on reality and partly on perception. You need to *do* the right things to impress them, because the professionals have ways of ferreting out the truth and are more objective than management tends to be. You also need to *say* the right things, because you're a prime source of information and you can sway their opinions. In other words, your strategy must be sound, but you must also have a sound strategy for selling it to your shareholders.

The share prices of many companies are lower than they should be because they don't have a strong, consistent story. Their messages are obscure and inconsistent. Investors struggle for facts and have to "decode" what's happening. They make assumptions without substance. Left to make up their own minds, they invent scenarios, strategies, and outcomes. In effect, they control the corporate future.

In good times, shareholders tolerate mistakes and don't fret if a company gets fat or inefficient, if productivity slumps, or if products aren't launched on time. But when the going gets tough, they pile on the pressure. When this happens, business leaders take flack. With their own earnings and jobs threatened, they are easily persuaded to do "what the market expects." The first response, more often than not, is to start cutting costs.

This may be essential, but it is seldom the only thing that needs doing. Even as you do it, you need to renew your focus on growth and do whatever you must to prepare for future growth. And you need to remind shareholders that it's easier to debilitate your company than preserve or build its capabilities, and that overaggressive surgery can kill the patient. Shrinking continually is no way to grow.

The bottom line is, if you don't have a compelling point of view, and if you fail to explain the logic of your strategy, you shouldn't be surprised that investors shy away or underrate your company. Strategic conversation influences them as much as anyone else.

MAKING A DIFFERENCE MAKES THE DIFFERENCE

In the new business arena, business models are being invented at light speed, making today's market leaders dinosaurs overnight. Prices and margins in most industries are being driven down to unattractive levels because too many competitors are chasing the same flighty customers. "Breakthrough" products and services are commoditized in the blink of an eye. So you can't get away from this reality: *as long as you look and act the same as others, you will be endangered. If your value proposition is just like everyone else's, there's no reason for customers to buy from you.*

If you don't make a difference, you don't matter!

In this cluttered, fast-moving world, when change and innovation are on everyone's lips, it's increasingly hard to stand out from the crowd—and harder still to stay apart and ahead. Little wonder, then, that branding is such a big deal. But that doesn't make it the answer to all your concerns. And it's a far more complex issue than most executives think.

Companies go to great lengths—and spend great fortunes—promoting their products and services as "New!" "Unique!" "Remarkable!" "Superior!" Mostly, they waste their money because they fail to create business models that are "New!" "Unique!" "Remarkable!" "Superior!" The result is predictable: they can't deliver what they promise, so they destroy their credibility.

A brand is not something you can get your hands around. Rather, it's the bundle of perceptions and feelings customers hold for a product, service, or company—or all three as a whole. And, while their views may be precise and intense while they're shopping or thinking about it, and less so at other times, the "system" that shapes those views is real. It's made up of people, machines, ideas, technologies, systems, philosophies, and much else.

It's the same with reputation management—another growth industry. While communications consultants, corporate image designers, and public relations people all have important roles in defining and promoting a company's image, they can ultimately do only what the underlying business model allows. For a while they might be able to create more excitement than a business deserves, but if the business falls short on delivery, their hype will hurt more than help.

THE FIRST PRINCIPLES OF BUSINESS COMPETITION

The business model that delivers jelly rolls is one thing; it takes another design to sell networking equipment or bulldozers. Within any industry there's likely to be a range of models. But, while every company should strive to be unique in the customer's mind, all have to build their strategies on the same basic principles. The First Principles of Business Competition apply to all (Figure 2-1).

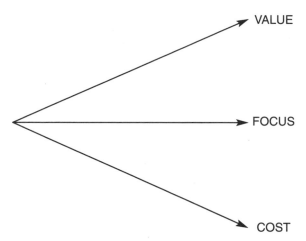

Figure 2-1 *The First Principles of Business Competition are Focus, Value, and Cost. They apply to every company, in every industry. If these aren't obsessions in your organization, it won't survive to fight for long. If they are, you'll beat a lot of competitors that may seem smarter or stronger.*

Winning and keeping customers depends 100 percent on them. Whatever you sell, and whomever you sell it to, you have to do these three things or you won't survive:

1. **Focus** your resources where you'll get the most from them.
2. Continually drive up your customer's perception of **value**.
3. Simultaneously drive down the **cost** of doing it.

These are obviously more than just marketing or branding issues. They are matters of *business design* and of *execution*. Apply these basic strategic principles, and your car, DVD player, sofa, savings plan, bottled water, tank top, ethical drug, or whatever has a chance of grabbing attention and customers. But deny the principles—or try something else—and you can be sure the good times won't last.

Focus is a decision that may be made by a few people in your organization, and holding your course is a leadership matter. But driving value up and costs down depends on *everyone*. Even if you alone—or a small group—make initial choices about *how* to do it (i.e., the processes), all the people on your team must apply themselves to the *doing*.

Their imagination and spirit enable you to "push the envelope" and take value delivery to new levels. Customer satisfaction becomes a moving target— which *you* move. Falling costs give you the margin you need for profit or a price war or to invest in further innovation and improvement, training, marketing, or whatever else you need to stay ahead.

As we'll shortly see, it's not just your own people who affect your results. Many other stakeholders may be involved. So you need to manage their involvement too, to be sure they help you implement the First Principles. Strategic conversation is the tool.

HARD CHOICES

It seems only yesterday that "sustainable competitive advantage" was every strategist's goal. Now, managers are told they should be grateful for even a brief lead over the thundering herd. This is hardly a surprise, given that things change so fast and that pretty much the same information is available to everyone at the same time.

In the 1960s and 1970s, long-range planners bet the farm on precise predictions of future outcomes. They got it wrong so often that scenario planning found a welcome audience in the next two decades. Executives fell in love with the idea of thinking about not just one future but several.

And there's merit in having more than "Plan A" in your briefcase; in fact, you should be nervous if you haven't also thought about "Plan B" and "Plan C." One reason is simply that it's smart to carry a parachute when you're flying into strange territory. But, more important, when you send your mind on a scouting trip, you get to mentally rehearse dealing with different situations so that if they arise, you've already "been there."

But don't think this lets you off the hook. No matter how many futures you imagine, you can't chase them all. Choose. If you don't bet, you never win.

Whatever industry you're in, and no matter how big or small your company may be, you have to decide where to focus your resources and how to use them. This is always risky, because things change and what looks like an attractive opportunity today may be worthless or a costly distraction tomorrow. Valuable resources can be blown through bad choices.

When you choose where to aim, you also choose where *not* to aim. When you choose how to move in a certain direction, you also choose how *not* to do it. So making choices always means shutting out possibilities, which is both an uncomfortable thought and a risk.

Commitment is crucial to success. The trouble is, some business commitments may be irreversible—or, at least, hard to walk away from. What's more, you may have to sign up today in the hope of a payday many years away into a future you can't see.

The most important resources you have are money and minds. Both are limited. If you're not clear where you'll apply them, if you try to protect yourself by doing a bit of this and a bit of that, you'll never be great at anything. If you don't apply *a critical mass of resources* to getting what you want, you'll fail. In this world, happy amateurs don't often win, and seldom more than once.

This is the reality that every manager faces, and most try to deny. "Spray and pray" strategies are common because they don't demand commitment. They're deadly for the same reason.

You can't cover yourself by betting on everything. You have to bet on *something*.

WINNING VOTES

Choosing where to go is one thing; to get there, you need plenty of help.

Some companies fail because they have lousy strategies. More often, *implementation* is the stumbling block. Managers can't turn their ideas into action. Planning is an annual rain dance, but wonderful plans don't necessarily bring rain. Usually, they turn to dust.

Strategy is clearly one of the most important issues on the top management agenda. But that doesn't mean it's exclusively a matter for top managers. The fact that they hog it in so many companies is precisely why it so often comes to nothing.

Implementation is a team affair. It involves not just insiders but many people outside, as well. Every organization has many stakeholders with different agendas. These are its "voters," and they choose whether it will move forward or backward or simply stand still.

Stakeholders fall into six groups:

1. **Company**—all insiders.
2. **Customers**—anyone who buys its products or services.
3. **Competitors**—"natural" ones who are in the same business, and others who compete for the same customer spending.
4. **Suppliers**—who provide whatever the business needs to function, including finance, services, supplies, components, and utilities.
5. **Influencers**—anyone who can make life easier or harder, such as activists, lobbyists, industry associations, the media, environmentalists, and trade unions.
6. **Facilitators**—those who make it possible to carry on the business, such as government, regulators, licensing agencies, and standards authorities.

Some stakeholders can fall into more than one group. Just where you put them isn't important; what does matter is that you accept that they all have some kind of interest in your success or failure, they all influence what you can do, and it's better to have them on your side than fighting against you or getting in your way.

Most of your stakeholders either can't or don't work as hard for your organization as they might. Because they don't understand your strategy or don't agree with it or feel the need to support it, they aim their energies elsewhere. In some cases, they may work actively *against* your company (Figure 2-2).

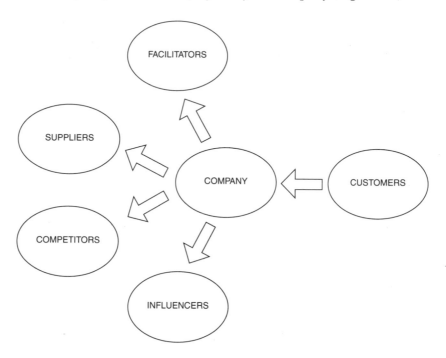

Figure 2-2 *Too often, companies and their stakeholders are in conflict. Their ambitions, intentions, and actions all diverge. Without alignment, energy is sprayed in all directions, and executives waste time trying to pull things together.*

This is a serious matter in an increasingly networked world. If you ever thought you had your value chain under control, that's probably not true today. Key players in your value system may be across town or on the other side of the globe. And when you cross them, they may take to the streets, boycott you, or "flame" you on the Internet.

A key objective in strategy is to get all that stakeholder energy focused on the same objectives (Figure 2-3). This multiplies the impact of their efforts and gives your organization "more bang for its bucks."

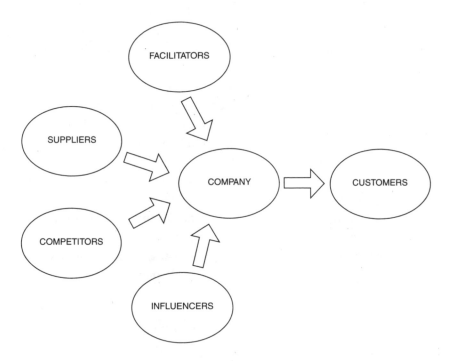

Figure 2-3 *When a company and its stakeholders face the same way, resources are focused and positive progress is likely. Singleminded, consistent communication is the key to getting your act together and concentrating your resources on critical goals.*

What's more, since innovation comes from many places, it brings unexpected ideas and insights to your management team. And you waste less time and energy arguing and sorting out differences.

While strategy is partly about making choices, it is largely about *communication.* Smart choices can give you an edge—but only if you sell them to your stakeholders and get their enthusiastic and active support.

Winning their votes begins with the way you create your strategy. There are two ways to go about it:

1. You can appoint a small team (usually of your most senior people) to create your strategy and then try to convince others that it's good for them.
2. You can involve more people from the start so that they understand both the big picture and the fine detail, the complications and the implications, and own the process and the outcomes.

Of course, you have to be practical. Too many cooks *can* spoil the broth. Big meetings *can* be counterproductive. Too many voices *can* result in noise, rather than clarity. There are questions of time and the availability of lots of people. And revealing your hand can be dumb.

On balance, however, you'll do best to err on the side of involving more rather than fewer people early in any change process. *Their participation equips them to perform. There is no way to make up for the learning that takes place when people work together on important tasks.*

To see how important this is, consider how value is created in new economy companies. It's a complex process, with multiple players.

A SYSTEMS VIEW OF VALUE DELIVERY

Most managers are familiar with the idea of a value chain. But a neat, linear unbundling of activities fails to capture the richness of what business must do to get results. In this time of environmental complexity, rapid change, globalization, temporary alliances, outsourcing, empowerment, e-commerce, and systems thinking, you need another, more holistic view.

Every company has to do five things to capture and keep customers and deliver consistent profits (Figure 2-4). Whether you're selling hot dogs or hedge funds, you have to:

1. Be alert to what's going on *outside* that may be an opportunity or a problem and to what is happening *inside* that might be either an advantage or a handicap (SENSING).

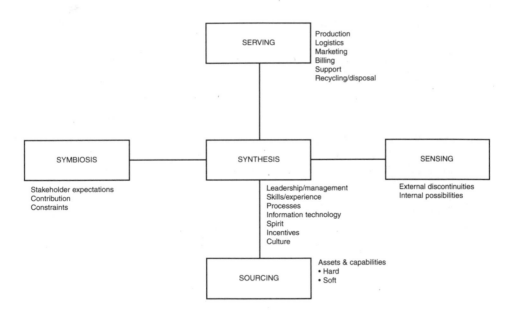

Figure 2-4 *Value is created and delivered through five essential activities. Each of them relies on the goodwill of your people. The central factor—synthesis—is the process by which you create a context for high performance and pull the other activities together.*

2. Acquire or build key resources—both "hard" ones like cash, raw materials, components, and so on and "soft" ones like skills, knowledge, brands, patents, reputation, etc. (SOURCING).
3. Create and deliver value to customers (SERVING).
4. Maintain win-win relationships and thus live in harmony with a wide range of stakeholders (SYMBIOSIS).
5. Pull it all together into a cohesive whole that is more than the sum of the parts (SYNTHESIS), and learn as you go.

The central issue in this model—synthesis—is obviously the most important one. For the critical key to competitiveness, and the most underrated, is the ability of managers to link insights and ideas, to draw together and align their assets, resources, and activities, and to connect their organizational capabilities to customer needs and wants.

Many companies don't survive, even though they understand their environment, have a lock on important resources, employ finely tuned service-delivery processes, and work hard at their relationships with their stakeholders. The reason, most often, is that *they can't get their act together*. Their various activities are not aligned, integrated, or mutually supportive.

Synthesis is a product of that most basic human activity: conversation. When people don't talk about the right things—and don't talk about them *constantly*, *creatively*, and *constructively*—things quickly come unglued. Parts of the organization come adrift, and resources are sprayed in different directions. On the other hand, when people are informed, involved, and encouraged to speak their minds, miracles happen.

Synthesis is most likely when people meet and talk face to face. So you should do everything possible to make this happen—and to make it easy. But technology is a terrific enabler. It can make information instantly and equally available to your whole team. It lets people make smarter decisions, provide better service, monitor performance, share ideas, and learn in real time.

Unfortunately, many businesses put technology ahead of people. They're easy prey for vendors promising "solutions," and they let the tail wag the dog. Their state-of-the-art systems don't talk to each other, let alone to the poor humans who're supposed to use them. They forget why they need their tech toys and keep buying more in the hope that sometime things will gel. And the big day just keeps moving further into the future!

So—back to basics. Decide first *what* you need to talk about, *who* needs to be involved (your own people, customers, suppliers, etc.), and *how* you might facilitate their conversation. Then—and only then—if you're sure information technology will help, go shopping. This way, you won't spend a cent before you need to, and when you do pull out your checkbook, you'll know exactly what you're about.

Apply the framework on page 33 to your discussions about value delivery, and you'll bring sense to questions about systems and structure. Ignore it, and "organizational architecture" will be a recurring nightmare.

STRATEGY AND SPIRIT

Every company needs a strategy. But in a world of constant surprises, competitive advantage often depends less on the choices you make than on *what you do about them*. How you act can make the difference between winning and losing—between life and death. Often, you have to move before all the facts are in, or before you can think through things as thoroughly as you'd like.

Effective execution is most likely when your goals, action steps, and methods are clear. These come from strategy. But there's another factor that's increasingly important in these hypercompetitive times—*the human spirit*.

Implementation is worth 100 IQ points!

If your company is to be a winner, your people must be alert to possibilities. They must also be passionate about what they do and enthusiastically invent their way into the future. It's your job as leader to focus them on the right "hill," but it's then up to them to apply their imagination and spirit to racing up the value path and down the cost path.

A lot is expected of them. They must not only be ready and able to change at a moment's notice; they must also apply great energy to making it happen. They must overcome all sorts of obstacles, cope with disappointment and failure, press on in the face of adversity and disappointment, and find new ways to deliver value and cut costs in the face of rising customer demands, relentless pressure, and shrinking deadlines. Work, in other words, is not all a breeze. Much of it is a chore and a bore.

And face it: they have choices. They can elect to perform like superstars or to goof off and save themselves for what really matters to them. If they don't find meaning in their work, they'll surely seek it elsewhere.

You can't force people to perform. The best you can do is create a context in which they will apply their minds and their efforts as *volunteers*, rather than *conscripts*, a context in which they want the same things as badly as you do and will bust a gut to get them. This is partly a matter of organizational culture ("the way we do things around here"). It is even more a matter of *climate* ("the way things feel around here—and the way *I* feel about being here").

As the following matrix shows, companies need to balance strategy and spirit (Figure 2-5). Too much or too little of one or the other will hurt results.

Which kind of company is yours?

- NO-HOPERS have no strategy, or it's a lousy one, and their spirit is weak.
- NERDS apply their minds to creating strategy that's precise and detailed. But they don't have the spirit to drive it, so it doesn't deliver the results they want.
- PARTYGOERS are hugely spirited but lack strategy. They are busy, busy, busy, but because they're directionless they flap around and go nowhere.
- PITBULLS are clear about where they're headed and ferocious about getting

there. They don't mess around, call for more research or another meeting, or talk endlessly in the hope that they'll get consensus; they just fix on a target and go for it!

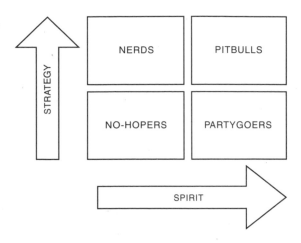

Figure 2-5 *Competitiveness demands both a clear strategy and a winning spirit. You should naturally strive for a strategy that's superior to anything your competitors may dream up. But even the best strategy in the world will have a short shelf life if it's not driven by extraordinary human spirit. If your people aren't passionate about your corporate quest, you're unlikely to either get ahead or stay there.*

It's tempting to see strategy and spirit as two separate issues. The one, after all, is about analysis and choices, the other about attitude. The first is a *task* (and as such can be delegated), while the second is a *mindset* that belongs to individuals and can be neither delegated nor commanded.

But wait a minute! What if strategy were a widely shared responsibility? What if it were "everybody's business," and of concern to more than a select few? What if more of your people understood your motivations and intentions?

Strategy and spirit are two sides of the same coin—*yin* and *yang*. When people are involved in making strategy—when it's "theirs"—they have a vested interest in its execution. If things change, they understand the background to the strategy and the nitty-gritty details, so they are able and likely to quickly adapt. What's more, the very fact that they were included in such a vital exercise is sure to motivate them. So strategy lights up their spirit!

My matrix illustrates why so many companies invest so much time, energy, and money in their strategies and get such dismal results. It also suggests that it's time for a new perspective on creating and holding competitive advantage. One that sees strategic management:

- as a *dynamic, living process*, and not a static product (i.e., a set of decisions or a document);
- as *an experiment*, with space for variety, mistakes, learning, and growth, rather than a precise, systematic technique;
- as *a deeply held belief in the value of individuals* as "scouts" who can greatly improve a company's early-warning capability and as creators who are blessed with the ability to think, imagine, adapt, and do extraordinary things;
- as *a leadership issue* that is too big for "leaders" alone.

For all the controversy about whether it works or not, strategic planning remains one of the most common management practices around the world. Planners may have vanished, but planning is alive and well. At the same time, the past two decades have seen more attention being given to the effective management of people in organizations. The "human resources school" has at last gained a fair hearing. Yet planning and people remain on separate tracks.

And rightly so, many would say. For only a few people are capable of thinking strategically. Only a few have the knowledge, the training, the experience, and the "big picture" view that enables them to take high-level decisions.

This "us and them" mindset ensures underperformance. It also ensures that when things change in the external environment, most companies change too slowly. Yesterday's ways are recycled again and again, when fresh thinking is desperately needed. Motivation is an ongoing problem. Little learning takes place. And bold plans come to nothing.

Companies everywhere complain of a shortage of "magic people." Yet they fail to acknowledge the talent they already have. They go out of their way to attract new people, when they already have people who are just aching to make a difference.

Of course, all your people won't all be equally keen to hear about the world around them. Nor will they all react to your communication and encouragement with great ideas or by working harder and being more cooperative. But *some* will surprise you. And in most companies, you need only a few more people who are positive and inspired to make a massive difference.

Their spirit is infectious. They become missionaries for your organization's success. They spread the word . . . and the mindset.

Contrary to popular myth, leadership is not a solo activity. For one thing, you need followers. But even more important, you need a critical mass of people around you who can think and act strategically—*who can make up their own minds and literally lead themselves.*

To achieve this, you have to break free of the quaint notion that it's enough to involve people—but only in decisions that affect their immediate tasks. You have to abandon the idea that participation is good—but only when you say so. And you have to forget about making some discussions off limits to "the masses." Instead, you have to promote a more widely dispersed sharing of information, responsibility, and power, plus total accountability. And you have to encourage the most rigorous, robust debate possible, to bring out the best in every member of your team.

> **To imagine that every person can be a brilliant strategist is pure nonsense. But to believe that they can't contribute is idiotic.**

STRATEGY IS CHANGE MANAGEMENT

Traditionally, strategy and implementation have been seen as different issues. First you *think*, and then you *do*. And this is precisely why execution comes unstuck.

The thinkers are from one group (up in the ivory tower, isolated from the hurly-burly of daily affairs). The doers are the rest—down in the dust and dirt (or maybe in sanitized cubicles), unaware of the big issues swirling around them, ignorant of the impact of what they do, paid to follow instructions.

As we've seen, neither group has line of sight to reality. Both are, to a greater or lesser extent, cut off from facts that could alter their perceptions and their actions.

Issues of macroeconomics, politics, society, and even competition are not seen or understood by the organization at large. Those at the top don't hear customer opinions or complaints or notice their changing demands and habits. Just about everyone is out of touch with the trends, events, and ideas that should be factored into strategy.

As long as strategy and change management are kept in different boxes, there will be a costly disconnect between them. But you can close the gap by thinking of strategy *as* change management.

Consider why that makes sense.

To make change happen, you have to do four things (Figure 2-6):

1. **Create dissatisfaction with the status quo.** This is the most important step and the one that's skipped over most often. But think about it: if a critical mass of people don't feel a real need to change, why should they change? Answer: they won't. They'll carry on as they are.

   How do you create that dissatisfaction? By flooding people with information. By exposing them to reality. By involving them in "big" conversations about what's going on inside and outside the organization and what it means. By asking how *they* see things.

---

2. **Debate possible futures.** People need to know what they're changing *to*. Usually there's more than one option. And the greater the number of people involved in this discussion, the more of them will start thinking in terms of *possibilities* instead of just impossibilities.

3. **Act to learn.** Until you *do*, you never know what you *can* do. Your grand visions remain mere theory. You learn nothing—about the world at large, or about your capabilities. Discovery is impossible. On the other hand, when you do snap into action and try something—*anything*—you quickly find out what works and what doesn't and you lay stepping stones for future progress.

4. **Review and revise.** From time to time, you need to pause and reflect on where you've been, what happened, and what might have been. This makes your *tacit* knowledge *explicit*, and it makes the knowledge of individuals available to everyone. If you don't do this deliberately, your understanding

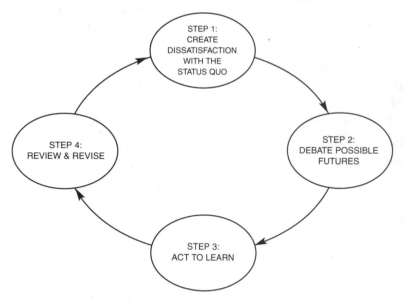

Figure 2-6 *Strategy and change management involve exactly the same steps. So to see them as separate activities is to set yourself up for failure in both.*

will be limited, your learning will be incomplete, and you will run the risk of doing more of the same long after it has become dangerous or dysfunctional to act that way.

The change cycle is a self-fueling engine: each step drives the next. So when you pause and take stock (Step 4), you're likely to see gaps in what you've done as well as reasons for new and more aggressive action. And that's almost sure to take you into a new phase of dissatisfaction.

Now think about the strategy process. It follows precisely the same cycle. You monitor and analyze your environment and your organization—which should create dissatisfaction. You debate your purpose and your possibilities and set priorities. You act on them and learn from the experience. You review progress and adjust course. And the cycle continues . . . .

Thus, strategy is change management: the two activities are in fact a single process. The disconnect between them that is such a problem in so many companies is by no means inevitable.

The cycle of change will speed up or slow down to match the heartbeat of the world. Sometimes you'll need to put your foot to the floor and cover a lot of distance fast. At other times, you can sensibly take it easier. It is just as foolish and unrealistic to try to travel flat out all the time as it is to go too slowly. The best pace is a matter of judgment, and the ability to set it is a key competitive strength. The best strategists are alert to the conditions ahead and flexible in their driving style.

ACTION LEARNING FOR CULTURE CHANGE

When the need for change of almost any kind is clear, most companies quickly latch on to the idea of changing their culture. They assume that when this happens—when people "get their attitudes right"—all will be well. But, once again, this is a back-to-front approach. And there's little chance it will deliver positive results.

The reason is simple. As psychologists have advised for more than 100 years, you don't change behavior by changing people's minds. *You change their minds by changing their behavior!*

Of course, companies have cultures. And of course, you might need a different culture from the one you have right now. But you can make change in your organization relatively easy or impossibly hard.

If you start by trying to "fix the culture," you're in for a tough time. For one thing, you have to decide what kind of intervention will deliver the culture you want (and you'll get a different answer from everyone you talk to, because they'll all promote their own "solutions"). Second, it'll take you so long to see an impact on sales and profits, you're likely to run out of steam and support. And finally, you have to have faith in the assumption that you can reengineer people's thinking "in the right direction" and that, when you do, they'll act the way you want them to.

The better option is to do what Alcoholics Anonymous does to help new members dry out: encourage them to drink less each day *this week*, so they can prove to themselves that it's possible . . . then another bit less next week . . . and the next week . . . until, one day, the habit is dead.

Your priority should be to change not what people *think* but what they *do*. That way, they'll discover that "the way we do things around here" is not cast in stone and that other ways work better. And, over time, your organization's culture will change.

Changing what they do is relatively simple. Inform people why new results are needed . . . set new goals . . . involve them in identifying priorities and creating action plans . . . get fast feedback . . . and review performance in a robust way.

This approach gives you two big wins:

1. *You get rapid performance improvement.* You see a positive difference in sales, costs, service levels, quality, and so on. And each success is a stimulus for the next.
2. *You get your intended culture change.* Instead of wasting time and money trying to convince people that they should work together, make better prod-

ucts, or go the extra mile for customers, now people decide for themselves that it's a good idea.

Most managers think about culture as a *cause* of behavior. In fact, it's also a *consequence*. Culture shapes behavior as much as behavior shapes culture. Understanding this is a key insight for strategists. It lets you shift from being a "victim" of culture to being its master; from having to wait for better results until your organization's culture changes to being able to drive better results and thus change your culture!

BEYOND CULTURE TO CLIMATE

If culture takes time to change, you can change the *climate* in your organization much faster. The "weather" determines how people feel at work. Make them comfortable, safe, and happy (also known as "hygiene factors"), and they're likely to add value. Ignore their basic needs and their feelings, and you'll bring out the devil in them.

The critical factor in any organizational climate is trust. When it's there, people share ideas, listen to each other, and rely on one another. When it's not, communication breaks down, they second-guess everything, and they doubt everyone. Unfortunately, while trust takes time to build, it can be destroyed in an instant.

Corporate climate (like almost everything else) is a consequence of strategic conversation. Nourishing conversation makes people feel good, and when they feel good they want to contribute. Toxic conversation makes them feel bad—a recipe for disaster. Nourishing conversation fosters trust; toxic conversation kills it.

If your company is performing well, chances are the climate is working for you. The challenge is to keep it that way. If, on the other hand, you've hit a bad patch, you need to deal carefully with the climate, or you could make things worse. When people sense panic, and when suddenly the conversation turns snappy, critical, or disrespectful, it's not long before distrust, fear, and poisonous hall talk follow.

Performance crises often creep up on businesses. But sometimes they occur with little warning. The economy swings sharply, customer spending freezes, competitor activity escalates, and prices tumble. Managers who were quite pleased with their results suddenly see a new picture on their radar screens. Triage is required.

At moments like this, it's tempting to be tough. The market is watching, after all, and the market likes decisive, bold action. But there are various options for administering whatever treatment is needed.

One is to surprise people with a cold announcement about cost cutting. You'll close so many plants, eliminate so many jobs, and so on. You're terribly sorry, but you have to do this for the sake of the survivors. After all, it's surely better to hand layoff notices to a few people now than to share the pain with everyone later . . . .

Another way is to ensure that people get whatever information will help them understand what's happening, what the options are, and why you have chosen a particular course of action and, at the same time, to remind them that, while you have to make the company leaner, you're doing it in pursuit of future *growth*. This won't take away the very real problems that will be experienced by those who are laid off, but it may lessen their anger and help them deal with the pain.

Best of all, of course, would have been a *proactive* approach in which people understood way ahead of any emergency how economic cycles work, what companies must do to survive, and what they personally must do to be survivors, an approach based on a strategic conversation that constantly emphasized growth but also stressed the need for careful cost management.

By creating a climate in which the facts are on the table, to be debated by everybody, you preempt trouble. You also make it more likely that you will avoid trouble in the first place.

RAISE YOUR ORGANIZATION'S "STRATEGIC IQ"

In this world of constant change, decisions must be made on the run. The alertness, imagination, spirit, and responsiveness of many people make the difference between winning and losing. No leader can call all the shots. Sensing, decision making, and responsibility for results have to be dispersed. People at all levels and in all functions have to be able to think and act strategically. The "strategic IQ" of your entire organization is, literally, a life-and-death factor.

Hiring well is obviously the first step in ensuring that your company has a critical mass of people who can make a difference. Ongoing training is essential. But neither of these building blocks will take you to the greatest heights.

Most valuable human development occurs in "the school of hard knocks," not in the classroom. Most people's growth and inspiration results from their day-to-day activities and interactions. The conversations they're involved in shape their attitudes and aspirations and impact on their capabilities. Yet, common practices ensure that too many individuals are constrained rather than liberated and that only a few are able to think and act strategically.

Structures, systems, and processes all get in their way. Corporate culture and management style can kill their initiative and block their performance and growth. *In effect, people are forced to shortchange their companies, because their companies cut them out of the conversational loop and limit what they can do and what they can become.*

While the "heavies" engage in a "big conversation" about the company's context, its challenges, its strategy, and so on, the majority of employees are allowed to take part only in a "small conversation" that focuses narrowly on their jobs, their specific tasks, the methods they use, and the results they must get (Figure 2-7).

The strategic IQ of most companies is pathetically low—*because of the way they make strategy.* But you can change that fast, by immediately involving as many people as possible in your company's "big conversation." This single step will do more than anything else to align and motivate your team members and to empower them to conquer tomorrow.

By creating a new climate in which individuals can decide for themselves what they need to know and how they should use information, you send a powerful signal about your trust and confidence in them. At the same time, you earn *their* trust, and they gain confidence in themselves. And, as your company's strategic IQ shoots up, so does its competitiveness.

This takes some planning and effort and a new approach to managing. But it needs no new budgets, no new training programs, no new compensation plans. In fact, it's free. Getting smart is the best business bargain ever.

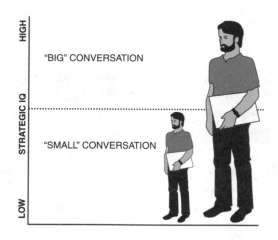

Figure 2-7 *If you want "management pygmies," restrict your people to "small conversations." On the other hand, if you want them to do extraordinary things—and if you want to raise your organization's "strategic IQ"— invite them into the "big conversations." They'll grow faster than you imagine—and they'll contribute more than you expect!*

THE QUEST FOR MEANING

Faced with the need to improve their competitiveness, most companies turn as if by instinct to new incentive plans. But to do this is once again to tackle the challenge from the wrong end. *First,* you need to change the way you manage people, *then* change how you reward them. If your management style is toxic, you'll never pay them enough. If it's nourishing, pay becomes secondary to doing great things.

If people are to be effective in any job—and certainly if they are to be exceptional at it—they need to know five things:

1. **What** to do (the task).
2. **Why** to do it (the context, the reason, the implications).
3. **How** to do it (the method).
4. **How well** to do it (standards).
5. How well they are **doing** (results).

In almost every company, most attention is given to "what" and "how." A growing number of companies are reasonably clear about "how well." But where most fall down is in helping people understand "why" and in giving them feedback on "how well they're doing."

Implementation is a massive problem not because people are idiots, don't want to work, or don't know what to do but rather because they don't know *why* their work is important.

All of us seek self-esteem and meaning in our lives. We need to know we matter. So we need to understand our context and the impact of getting things right or doing them wrong. And we need open and honest—and *regular*—feedback so that we know where we are and how we're performing and when to change course.

This is an age of talent wars. The best and the brightest are worth a fortune. It makes no sense to hire anyone less. But to *make* people less than they could be is a major commercial crime.

Magic people may for a while buck the odds and fight the system to do magical things. But, sooner or later, a lousy context will get them down and drive them away. So creating and sustaining a *magical context* is essential. This is the leader's task—and a consequence of the way you do strategy.

NEW ASSUMPTIONS

Strategic thinking hinges on your assumptions about the business arena and what works in it. Remarkably, though, no one seems in the least concerned about a most important question:

What are your assumptions about strategy?

What is strategy all about? What is its purpose? Why does it matter? What must you do to make it worthwhile? Whose responsibility is it?

If you don't think about these matters, you'll waste your time talking about strategy. You'll keep experimenting with new concepts and techniques because you won't have a point of view about what you actually need to do. And your chances of creating and implementing a sound strategy will be about zero.

The common view of strategy is that it's an occasional top management exercise that results in a plan that gets turned into orders that are passed down the line by decree. But this chapter has suggested another way of looking at it:

Assumption #1 **Strategy must prepare your organization to deal with an uncertain future.** You can't see precisely what lies ahead. You *will* be surprised. So your team's "strategic IQ"—its ability to sense and adapt to change—will make or break you. The process of creating and implementing strategy should be a learning activity that equips people to think and act effectively and that develops capabilities for the future.

Assumption #2 **Strategy is change—a process, not a plan.** It's not "done" when you finish your workshop or get the consultant's final report. It can't be driven by dates on your calendar. It's an everyday, ongoing process.

Assumption #3 **The First Principles of Business Competition are mandatory.** Every company must (1) *focus* its resources, (2) drive customers' perceptions of *value up*, and (3) drive *costs down*. No organization will get anywhere by trying to be all things to all people or by driving costs up and value down!

Assumption #4   **Imagination and the human spirit drive performance.** Business is a human endeavor. Good intentions must be turned into hard actions rapidly and effectively, in very challenging circumstances. While you may get some things done by issuing orders, many changes must be driven "from the fringes." You'll achieve greatness only if people on your team *volunteer* their imagination and spirit—if *they* detect new possibilities, inspire new ideas, and set new standards of performance.

Assumption #5   **Synthesis is the most important competitive skill.** Your ability to make connections—to "pull things together"—is what ultimately makes the difference between success and failure. If you can't do this, your stakeholders and your goals will pull your organization apart. If you get it right, synergy will become a reality and your company's capabilities will be multiplied many times over.

Assumption #6   **What's talked about is managed and measured.** If you don't have a clear point of view about where you're going, you shouldn't be surprised that no one follows you or supports you. Your "strategic conversation" must be deliberately crafted, clear, and well communicated, or people will do their own thing. And it must be managed on an ongoing basis, to keep things on track and to maintain the momentum.

The planning process described in this book is based on these assumptions. Now that we have the background, let's look at the way ahead.

3
PROCESS

PROCESS

S o you need a new strategy. Where do you begin? What process should you use? Which concepts should you apply? How can you be sure of taking into account all the factors that may impact on your performance . . . and turn your fine intentions into results?

For answers, let's look at the abilities you need to be a winner and why you have to be clear and convincing about your "business logic." Then we'll analyze your business environment in a brand new way and use a five-step process for creating your strategy. Finally, we'll move into action with a 30-day planning and review cycle that will ensure you get fast results.

A QUESTIONING PROCESS

Strategy is about asking questions. Meaningful strategic conversation requires rigorous probing into what your organization does, why, and how.

The first answer to any question is rarely the best answer. Taking things for granted in business is dangerous. Glib assumptions can kill a company. Board members earn their keep when they push and probe and dig until they get down to the bedrock of issues. Executives become effective when they do the same.

The questioning process needs to be tough. Debate about the answers must be robust. People need to know that whatever they put on the table will be taken apart (and that *they'll* be shredded if they waste others' time by being careless about what they share).

This dissection can be irritating and stressful to those in the spotlight. But it forces them to think through what they say. When they know that their views will be seriously tested, they do the "pretesting" themselves. They prepare better. They take into account issues they might otherwise gloss over. And they develop their arguments knowing that other people must feel equally comfortable with them.

The process also needs to be *respectful*. Its goal is not only to search for truth and insights but also to develop your team's confidence and strategic IQ and the members' trust in each other. So, while people should stick to the point, they should also be given enough time to make their point. Their ideas should get a fair hearing. They should feel free to say what needs to be said and not just stick to the party line.

The tone of every management conversation creates a context for the next one. Over time, you should aim to make your company's strategic conversations more focused, more challenging, more stimulating, and more creative. The benefits will be immense. You and your colleagues will gain in many ways, and your company 's competitive edge will be honed to razor sharpness.

In a frenetic business environment, with competitors falling over each other for space and racing for advantage, executives need to unclutter their thinking and cut swiftly to the heart of matters. If you use complex tools to think about your strategy, you will be unlikely to use them for long. Nor will they give you the results you need.

Simplicity is a powerful weapon. Simple questions are the essence of strategy making.

SIX ABILITIES THAT GIVE WINNERS THE EDGE

To start the questioning process, consider the six abilities every company must develop to be competitive (Figure 3-1). And think carefully about how you see your own organization.

Ability #1: Strategy making. "Do we understand our challenges and do we have a clear view of how we must respond?"

Ability #2: **Possibility thinking.** "Do we think 'out of the box' about what *could be*, rather than what *is*, or what is *impossible*?"

Ability #3: **Winning stakeholder support.** "Do we actively seek to win 'votes' through strategic conversation?"

Ability #4: **Business model design.** "Have we designed our organization to deliver the results we want?"

Ability #5: **Implementation.** "Do we have what it takes to meet our ambitions, and will our practices deliver the results we expect?"

Ability #6: **Learning and change.** "Are we alert to what's happening around us, and do we learn and change fast enough?"

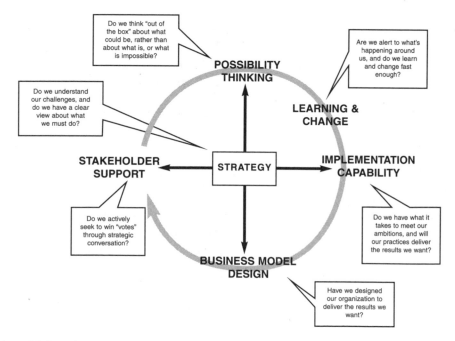

Figure 3-1 *Strategic management is an ongoing process of thinking, design, action, learning, and adjusting. The old view of planning-then-doing is obsolete. Today, these activities are all part of everybody's business, every day.*

Rate your organization on a 1–5 scale in each of these areas (where 1 is weak and 5 is strong). How do you fare? Don't kid yourself. Applaud your strengths, by all means, but own up to your weaknesses. That way, you'll see where you're vulnerable, and you'll know what to work on.

As with most of the questions we need to ask, these are all simple ones. But few managers can respond to them with a confident "yes." They hunt for sophisticated reasons why they don't perform, when the answers are staring them in the face.

DOES YOUR BUSINESS LOGIC ADD UP?

There are countless ways to succeed in business. Some produce better results than others by almost any measure: innovation, sales, market share, profits, longevity, or whatever. Executives worldwide use roughly the same management ideas. Yet surprisingly few of them are clear about what makes their companies successful. When they try to explain the formula, they're vague and unconvincing. And it doesn't take a genius to see that their "unique" competitive advantage is just like many others and will lead them straight down the commodity track.

When outsiders such as investors, analysts, or business journalists evaluate a company, they ask quite obvious questions (often implicitly rather than explicitly). Insiders, by contrast, seldom ask the same things. Worse still, they spend time on fluffy mission or values statements, make decisions based on assumptions rather than facts, and arrive at goals so vague they don't matter. The result is, they either can't explain their business logic, or, if they try, it doesn't add up.

Here are the critical questions (Figure 3-2):

1. **Is there a real—and *exploitable*—business opportunity for *this* organization?**[*]
2. **Is the business purpose clear and worth supporting?**
3. **Is there a "business recipe," is it spelled out, and is it likely to deliver the intended results?**
4. **Have hard choices and tradeoffs been made about priorities and actions?**
5. **Are essential resources and capabilities available, or can they be acquired or built?**

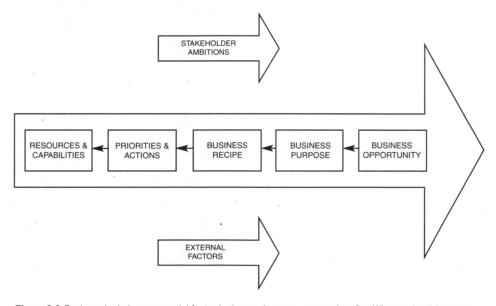

Figure 3-2 *Business logic is an essential factor in the war for customers and profits. What you're doing must make sense. When it all adds up, you can expect good results. When it doesn't—and too often it doesn't—you shouldn't be surprised that things go awry.*

[*] Every opportunity is not for everyone. Every customer is not "right" for every company. Some are worth chasing, while others should be left to someone else. Pick your fights and your targets careful-ly—and pick the ones you can win. Walking away is often the smart thing to do.

When the answers are connected by a straight line, the chances of success go up; when there are disconnects, danger lights should flash. Enthusiasm is no substitute for common sense.

But there's more. Companies don't operate in isolation. They are, to a real extent, "prisoners of their environment." So two other questions must be asked:

6. **Does this organization satisfy the ambitions of key stakeholders?**
7. **Does its strategy take into account external forces that may affect it?**

How does your business logic add up? Are your views based on fact? Do you *believe* what you're saying? Can you *defend* it? Will others—shareholders, suppliers, customers—buy it? Would you back your story with your own money?

A lot of executives—especially entrepreneurs with new ideas—are on shaky ground when they explain their strategies. Their PowerPoint presentations and spreadsheets may dazzle their audience, and their confidence may be compelling. But switch off the projector, turn up the lights, and apply the test of these seven questions. Suddenly, things look different.

There's nothing worse than a skeptic who can't see the promise of the future. But in the new economy there's no shortage of dreamers. And for all their hype, most will go down in smoke because they just don't make sense.

Who are you kidding?

These are exciting times, and the race is on to develop the business models of the future. Startups have to offer something new and different to break into already crowded markets. Established businesses must innovate just to stay in place. And growth for everyone will get harder as more competitors chase the same customers. But *beware of infatuation with "new rules" when the old ones still apply.*

Business life cycles are not dead—they're just shorter, and they're as much a product of flaky *thinking* as of poor *execution*. Strategies don't have to be brilliant; they do need to make sense. Being radical is no substitute for being rigorous; blend the two, and you're most likely to have a winner.

THE BIG TEST

One strategy question underpins all others:

On what assumptions do you base your thinking?

This is the killer probe. Time and again, executives come off the rails right here, because their assumptions are not clear—*even to themselves*. Yet they make assertions as if they were facts:

> "The economy will grow by 4 per cent this year."
> "Margins will definitely improve."
> "Our competitors are asleep."
> "Their only option is a price war."
> "No one is interested in this market; we have it to ourselves."
> "Our customers love us."
> "Our costs are the industry benchmark."
> "Our capabilities will let us compete anywhere."
> "We're world class."

But ask, "Do you *know*, or are you *guessing*?" and you'll see they're on shaky ground. They don't really know, they haven't checked, and more often than not they're saying what they like to think or what they imagine you want to hear!

Many things in business are a mystery. You can never get enough information, and often facts are slippery. What's more, things change. So you can be utterly certain of something today, only to find it untrue tomorrow.

The future is the greatest mystery of all. There is no way to know for sure how it will evolve. Futurists have a terrible record.[1] They get things wrong more often than they're right.

> **No risk, no reward.**

Management is about making bets on the future. The question is, *which future*? If hindsight is a perfect science, foresight is partly a matter of homework and largely a matter of luck. Gathering facts, speculating, and creating scenarios is no guarantee of success. Sometimes you'll get it right and often you'll be wrong.

It's obviously important to know as much about your environment as you can. Two frameworks bring order and discipline to the process and ensure that you consider all issues that might matter (Figure 3-3). The first one focuses on the drivers of competitive hostility in your domain. It looks at why the players in that arena act the way they do and helps you anticipate what they might do next. The second one gives you a more complete understanding of the world in which you all operate. It helps you develop a fine-grained picture of your world and the players and forces at work in it. And it asks a vital question: "Who gets the value?" (If the answer is not *you*, start plotting some changes!)

Before you tackle the questions posed in either of these frameworks, you need to draw a line around the business arena in which you work. Start with a broad-brush view and then narrow down your target this way:

- **Industry.** Some hip folk think it's unfashionable to talk in terms of "industry" (steel, motor assembly, bulk chemicals, retail banking), and prefer to talk about "space" (as in, "We compete in the nutraceutical space"). There's also a trend toward thinking about "white space" (unoccupied territory) between industries. These are hardly revolutionary ideas. You might well operate in two or more industries at the same time, but say so. That way, analysts and other important outsiders will know what you mean. (And *you'll* know what you mean!)

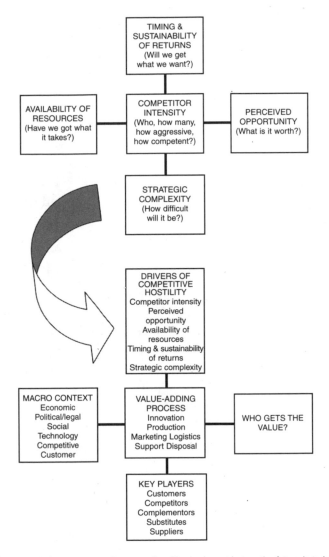

Figure 3-3 *The best way to improve your chances of making a decent bet on the future is to have an in-depth understanding of the world in which you compete. You need to understand both what causes competitors to act the way they do and what's happening in the macro arena.*

- **Geography.** Where, exactly, on this planet do you compete—or intend to compete? If you're "going global," which regions and countries will you include? Which areas within them (provinces, cities, towns, communities) will you concentrate on?
- **Product/customer category.** Specify what you sell, and to whom (household cleaner to career women, accounting software to small business, components to auto makers). What want or need do you satisfy? Where are you on the price scale? Do you provide "plain vanilla," or all the bells and whistles? How do people use your product or service?
- **Purchase and usage occasion.** When do people buy and use your offering? (If the buyer and the user are different, say so.)
- **Distribution method.** What distribution channels do you use? Who controls them?

The point of the exercise is to be clear about which turf concerns you and which doesn't. Doing this narrows your focus and lets you decide what you must deal with and what you can ignore. The more specific you are, the better. Beware, however, of being so neat and precise that you push potential competitors—or other factors—off your radar screen. Threats and opportunities come from unexpected places. If you're not alert, you may not see them till it's too late.

(For example, if you sell clothing, your biggest competitor may be mobile phones. If you sell cars, your customers' service expectations may be shaped not by other car companies but by airlines, restaurants, or the drycleaner down the road. If you operate a chain of cinemas, your most serious challenge may be from sports, PC games, downloaded music, or bookstores.)

No company can compete everywhere or be everything to everybody. You need to understand your territory, not the whole map. And you have to balance where you are now with where you want to be in the future.

You also have to decide how much information is "enough." Most companies know less than they should about their environment. Some are junkies who go overboard in their efforts to collect and analyze information. Effective leaders know when to call a halt and say, "Move on!"

No matter how thorough you are, you'll never take all the risk out of your decisions or be sure you're doing the right things. No amount of data gathering or number crunching will guarantee success. The futurist has not been born who can tell you what lies ahead. The best you can do is make an educated guess. Time will tell whether you got it right or wrong.

Environmental scanning is not just an exercise to improve your understanding of the world. It is not something to be done from time to time. And it is not something that should be left to a few people.

These frameworks should be central to an ongoing conversation between as many of your people as possible. By engaging many "scouts," your chances of seeing trends or shifts are greatly improved. Involving people in discussions about the environment usually makes them realize they're not happy with the status quo. And participation makes them aware that there are many views of the world and many possible futures—which prepares them to deal with a range of "tomorrows."

This is a key activity in a continuous process of change and growth. It gives you a good chance of seeing opportunities and problems early enough to act on them. It is also a *catalyst* for change, in that when people think about the world around them they almost always see the need for change. And it has a powerful *educational* effect, so it develops your team's strategic IQ.

As you debate the issues in these frameworks, keep asking that crucial question: "Do we *know*, or are we *guessing*?" And beware of letting assumptions slide into your analysis disguised as truths. Fooling yourself may make you comfortable in the short run, but sooner or later it will hurt you.

A SYSTEMATIC APPROACH TO PLANNING

Most strategic planning processes follow roughly the same path—and yield less than satisfying results. Yesterday's techniques are not likely to produce radical strategies. So here's a new approach that gets you thinking about your organization and its prospects in a more effective and practical way. It applies as much to a startup venture as to an established business; as much to successful organizations that wish to stay that way as to troubled companies in need of critical care.

There are five building blocks (Figure 3-4). Each requires that you answer a crucial question. Each of those, in turn, is answered through four further questions, which we'll get to shortly.* Here are the big five:

1. **Why do we exist?**
2. **How do we make money?**
3. **What kind or organization should we be?**
4. **What must we do, and how will we make it happen?**
5. **How will we win the support of our stakeholders?**

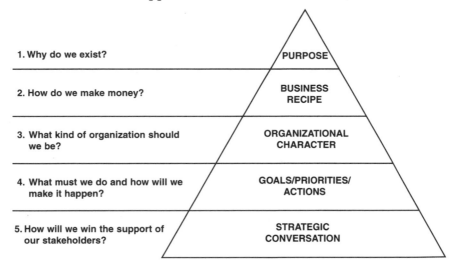

Figure 3-4 *Five questions give you a framework for thinking about your strategy. But, remember, you need to know what's happening around you as you make these decisions.*

---

* The full list is on page 85.

The "strategy pyramid" produces the answers that analysts and investors want. It guides you through a debate about where you intend to go and how. It also helps you think about the kind of organization you need in order to achieve your dreams.

STEP 1: DEFINE YOUR PURPOSE

Walk around almost any organization, and you'll hear people at all levels asking questions like these:

> "What are we trying to do?"
> "Where is this company going?"
> "What are the priorities?"
> "What must I focus on?"

Senior executives don't hear these concerns. Though only a few people at the top know more or less what the company's agenda is, they assume everyone else does, too. And they often get irritated when confronted with these "idiotic" questions. "That's ridiculous!" they fume. "Aren't they listening? What's wrong with people?"

Leadership is about providing direction. It's also about shaping the context in which people can make up their own minds, apply their own creativity, and make effective decisions (a context, in other words, in which they are *empowered*). If you could get away with a command-and-control style 20 or 30 years ago, today you can't. Environmental uncertainty, complexity, and accelerating change make it a killer. Without lots of thinking people doing their own thing and moving in roughly the same direction, your company just won't progress.

When there's confusion about direction, resources are wasted. Ad hoc decision making becomes a way of life. People with too little information do whatever seems smartest at the time, and they get it wrong a lot of the time.

Whatever strategy the bosses might have had in mind is ignored or quickly overtaken and blown apart by events. The business's agenda is decided in a random and haphazard way—literally by accident.

Your business purpose answers the question "Why do we exist?" It's framed, in turn, by these four questions (Figure 3-5):

1. **Whom do we serve?** Who are your customers? What other stakeholders must you consider? How do you rank them, so you know how to make tradeoffs between their competing demands?

2. **What value do we deliver?** What do customers get from a relationship with you? What products or services do you sell? What is your "difference"? What do you do for stakeholders who are not customers?

3. **Why do we matter?** Why is your existence important to your stakeholders? Why are they better off for having you around? Why should they support you? What would it mean to them if you disappeared?

4. **What is our ambition?** Where are you headed? What are you striving for? What do you want to achieve? By when?

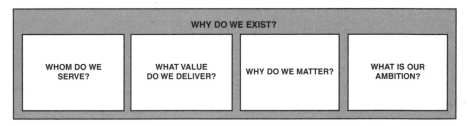

Figure 3-5 *Purpose provides direction and "stretch."*

Clearly, these questions are close to those that define a company's vision and mission. However, those terms have been badly abused and are too often confused. By focusing on a single notion—your purpose—you get straight down to business and to the decisions that will really make a difference.

STEP 2: DEFINE YOUR BUSINESS RECIPE

This is the area where companies come unstuck. Ask a team of managers separately how they make money, and they will tell you different things. Ask people elsewhere in the organization, and you'll get many answers—or blank stares. Ask, "Does all this make sense?" and the answer is usually "No!"

If your business recipe isn't clear, you can't expect your team to do the right things. Nor will your stakeholders support you.

Again, four questions provide the direction you need (Figure 3-6):

1. **What is our difference?** What is your value proposition to customers? What makes it unique? Why does it matter to them? (Think in terms of your *company* and its *products* and *services*; after all, customers buy the whole package.)

2. **How do we deliver our value proposition?** What business model underpins it?

3. **What makes our strategy superior?** It's too easy to say, "Of course we're best." But why? What gives your strategy the edge when every competitor thinks about roughly the same things, in much the same way . . . when they all have access to similar capabilities and face the same constraints . . . and when customers are increasingly smart and shopping around?

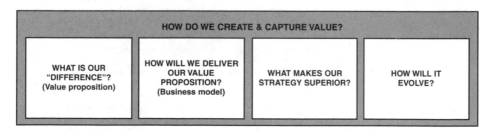

Figure 3-6 *The business recipe explains growth.*

4. **How will it evolve?** A critical and usually overlooked question. Many strategies work in the short term but quickly peter out or lead down a blind alley. Executives commit resources without thinking about the move after next. Best you talk about this up front so that, when you act, you do so with a clear view of where you're going.

DESIGN YOUR BUSINESS MODEL

The race for the future will be a race between competing business models. Dotcom frenzy is driven by the imagination of entrepreneurs who cook up new ways to sell everything from beans to banking. Yet established companies pay surprisingly little attention to this issue.

As we saw in Chapter 1, companies experience life cycles because they become good at doing something but keep doing it long after customers have grown bored and gone shopping elsewhere. And, given that so many competitors attack every opportunity, those life cycles are shrinking. Business models become obsolete in no time at all. Today's invaluable skills, technologies, and processes can become tomorrow's corporate killers.

Designing an effective business model requires that you think about the value-adding potential of a number of key building blocks, both separately and together. The 7Ps framework gives you a holistic view of your organization (Figure 3-7).[2] It prompts you to think about factors that are easily overlooked, yet that may be pivotal in creating and holding your competitive advantage.

As its name suggests, there are seven areas for inquiry. Your goal should be to outperform your competitors in each of them. Add up enough positive differences, and you'll be hard to catch. You'll gain even more advantage if you get the seven elements to lock together, to reinforce one another into a whole that is greater than the sum of the parts.[3]

(The downside is that while it may be hard to change one part of your model in the future, it'll be even harder when they're entwined. So the challenge is to

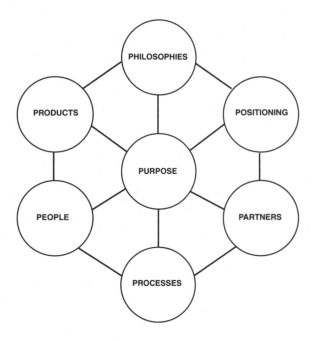

Figure 3-7 *The future of business will be dominated by a race for tomorrow's business models. The 7Ps framework gives you a comprehensive picture of your organization's current health and provides a starting point for thinking about new ways to compete.*

create a "tight" model—and at the same time to build in flexibility [Figure 3-8]. Once again, strategic conversation is a crucial factor.)

As with all the frameworks in this book, there are two ways to use this one. One is to look at the way things are now, so you get a comprehensive picture of your current business model—"Where we are today." The other is to explore possibilities for improvement and innovation—"Where we want to be tomorrow." And, of course, you can apply the framework in the same way to analyze your competitors, to probe for differences between you and them, and to identify areas of opportunity.

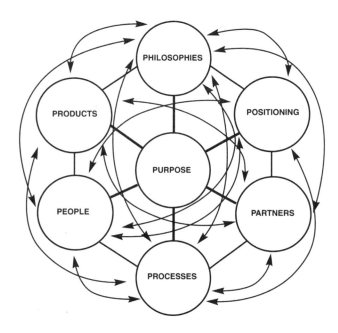

Figure 3-8 *You may gain an advantage by good design or implementation in any of the seven Ps. But the more differences you develop, the better. And the tighter the elements of your model link together, and the denser the connections, the harder it is for competitors to copy you.*

Here are the questions:

1. What is your business PURPOSE? This is the central issue. It frames each of the others and is in turn given life by them. Notions of vision and mission are still popular but mostly are of little help to managers, for they lead to struggles with words and conflict over where the commas should go. Your purpose is your "hill"—the place you want to reach—as well as your reason for being. It's the true north on your corporate compass, your inspiration, and your guide. (The questions on page 64 help you define your purpose.)

2. What are your PHILOSOPHIES? This question examines your views about

"the way we do things around here": from customer service to the types of people you hire and how you treat them; from cost management to your attitude about investing in research and development; from outsourcing to e-commerce; and so on. Because managers seldom question their underlying beliefs about such things, they don't agree on a stance, and their people have to keep asking for guidance. Unlike values, philosophies provide the pathways for your business decisions, so thinking about them deliberately, and making them explicit, is fundamental to the empowerment of your people.

3. What PRODUCTS (or services) do you sell? What makes them different and preferable? How hard is it to copy or improve on them? What substitutes might customers consider?

4. What is your chosen POSITIONING in the marketplace for your company and its offerings—that is, what market niche do you aim at, and how do you distinguish yourself? What makes this positioning unique and special? How do you promote it?

5. What kinds of PEOPLE do you hire? How do you recruit, induct, develop, measure, reward, and manage them for optimum performance?

6. What PARTNERS help you reach your goals? How do you identify them? What kinds of arrangements—formal or informal—do you enter into with them? How do you manage your relationships with them? How do you share costs and rewards?

7. What PROCESSES drive your performance? How do you do everything, from making and implementing strategy to administration, production, marketing, delivery, and disposal? What processes do you rely on for effective corporate governance? How do you measure performance? How do you communicate, internally and externally?

The 7Ps are the substance of your value proposition. They give it muscle and make your "brand" meaningful. Therefore, your business model needs to match the needs of your customers, and you must be able to renew it to keep pace with them and to stay ahead of your competitors. But your model also needs to be *commercially viable*: it must make sense, it must be affordable and workable, and it must cost less than it delivers.

STEP 3: CLARIFY YOUR ORGANIZATIONAL CHARACTER

If your company is to stand out, your people must do extraordinary things. But their efforts must be aligned. They must also occur within agreed bounds, for while it's exciting to think that "anything goes," trouble is likely to follow when there are no rules or values to guide behavior.

Since organizations are human groups, it's helpful to think about their human characteristics. Do this deliberately, and you may avoid having things happen by default. You'll also guide your people toward doing what's most likely to benefit your company, and so take the first important step toward empowering them.

What describes your company's character? What *should* describe it? How should people behave?

Here are the questions that lead to the answers you need (Figure 3-9):

1. **What assumptions guide us?** What beliefs underpin your behaviors? By digging down to the bedrock beneath your actions, you'll possibly uncover some of the reasons you fail to do the things you should do—or why you do the things you shouldn't.

2. **What turns us on?** What excites you, inspires you, and gets your juices flowing?

3. **What is not negotiable?** Every organization has some no-no's. These are the out-of-bounds areas where people can't go, the issues that can't be raised, the actions that won't be tolerated. What are yours?

4. **How do we behave?** What describes your organization's day-to-day conduct? How do people tackle projects, problems, challenges, and crises, relate to one another, deal with outsiders, manage "housekeeping" issues, and so on?

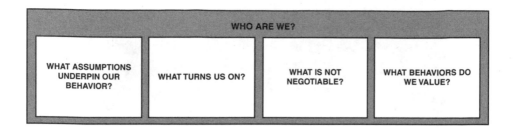

Figure 3-9 *Character defines the organization in human terms.*

STEP 4: DEFINE YOUR GOALS, PRIORITIES, AND ACTIONS

In the final analysis, the test of an executive comes down to the choices you make and what you make of them. You obviously want to pick wisely. But you also have to get things done.

When managers work on their to-do lists, they usually include too many items. But without hard choices, you'll never make progress. You might do the interesting things—and the ones clamoring for attention—but you probably won't do the *right* ones. Even if you do set out facing the right way, you'll likely wind up in the wrong place because you have too much on your plate.

Since every company has multiple stakeholders and must apply resources in various areas, concepts like the balanced scorecard have become commonplace. But many businesses struggle to use them effectively. In no time at all, they find themselves bogged down in endless debates and with action plans that lead nowhere.

Effective execution begins with having a clear, limited agenda. Anything else is asking for trouble. You need some goals, but, perhaps even more important, you need *priorities*. These are the few things that will make the big difference—the *must*-do's, not the *nice*-to-do's. (Remember the 80/20 rule?)

> **Every company has too much to do and too few resources. So you have to make choices and tradeoffs. You have to say "no" to many attractive possibilities. You have to take stuff *off* your agenda.**

Most companies have anywhere from eight to twelve performance drivers, or "headline" issues, on which they must deliver results. These obviously vary from company to company. For one organization, technology may be a big issue. For another, the environment or community relations matter more. A manufacturer might include quality, while a distribution business might focus on systems or alliances.

Now think of these key issues as the spokes of a wheel. The eight that are shown on the example below demand special attention from most companies (Figure 3-10). When you make your own choices, be sure that, whatever issues you decide on, they're the ones that make a life-or-death difference to *your* business. The point is to shorten the list, to hone in on the ones that will make the most difference, and to sideline the rest.

(Note that *innovation is not a separate issue*. The reason is, it matters in all of them. And the only way to change results in any area is through innovation. Nor is there a headline for "learning and change"—because, once again, these must happen everywhere.)

For clarity, here's what you might include under each headline issue:

1. CUSTOMERS—Market share, marketing activities (branding, promotions, pricing, sales, distribution), customer service, customer retention, sales value per customer.
2. QUALITY—Measurable and perceived standards in products and services, as well as the organization's overall performance.
3. PRODUCTIVITY—Output per person, per machine, per unit of money or time.
4. PARTNERS—All stakeholder relationships.

---

5. ORGANIZATION—Internal issues such as structure, systems, technology, and people.
6. PRODUCT—Current products, new product development, improvement, and line extensions.
7. FINANCIAL—Use of capital, balance sheet structure, revenues, costs, margins, debtors and creditors, profits and returns.
8. PROCESSES—Innovation and improvement in the value-delivery system.

Figure 3-10 *Your "strategy wheel" highlights the "headline" issues you must manage. It also shows that, while some issues may be in conflict with others, you have to balance them and manage all of them.*

Now, with your own "strategy wheel" in front of you, use the following questions to develop your action plan (Figure 3-11):

1. **What results do we seek?** What big goals do you want to reach within your planning period (which may be very short or several years long)? What subgoals are important? What must you achieve in the short term in order to deliver a long-term result?

2. **What are the priorities?** On what few high-impact issues must you concentrate your resources to achieve your goals? Since you can't do everything, what must you do *first*, and in what order must you tackle other things?

3. **What action must we take?** What specifically must you *do* about each of those priorities to get where you want to go? (There may be several actions, by different people, for any priority.)

4. **What must we do in the next 30 days to get started, and who is responsible?** Many things can't be finished quickly, but they can be *started*. What must happen today, tomorrow, or by the end of next week to remove any chance of "wheel spin"—an enemy of progress—and to demonstrate progress? And whose name must appear next to each action? (Usually, teams make things happen, but be sure to make *individuals* accountable.)

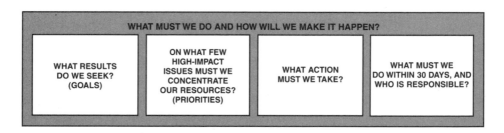

Figure 3-11 *Priorities and actions focus attention on high-impact tasks.*

The purpose of this process is to convert your "wish list" into one you can get your hands around and act on (Figure 3-12). It also forces you to discard many issues that might otherwise compete for your attention. Used systematically, it

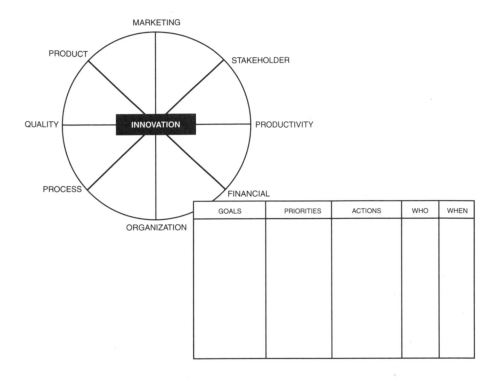

Figure 3-12 *Why reinvent the wheel? After all, it's a pretty good device for showing that every business must have a range of goals! It also lets you show that, while your goals may conflict with one another, you do need to manage all of them or your wheel will wobble. And, by creating 30-day action plans for each goal, you can drive performance rapidly through your company.*

will take you through a process of identifying the must-attend-to issues, deciding what to do about them, defining the outcomes you expect, assigning responsibility for action, and making a fast start.

Does this mean that the issues you choose are the only issues you must pay attention to? Of course not. But, you hope, they're the ones that matter most.

These are the ones you want on your 30-day action plans (the final step in the planning process) for regular review. There may well be other matters that you must keep an eye on, think about, and even act on sooner or later, but right now you need to choose and commit.

STEP 5: CRAFT YOUR STRATEGIC CONVERSATION

So you know where you're going. You know what your value proposition is and how you'll deliver it, you have a view on how you want people to behave, and you have your priorities and actions clearly before you. It's time to mobilize your stakeholders. It's time to bring your strategic conversation into sharp focus.

This is where your earlier conversations—and all the analysis, insight, imagination, inspiration, and good intentions they produced—turn into commitment and action . . . or wasted opportunities, frustration, and losses. This is where the winners are separated from the also-rans.

Here are the key questions (Figure 3-13):

1. **Whom must we talk to?** Who is the audience? Which stakeholders must you address, inform, and persuade?
2. **What do they need to know?** Everyone doesn't need to know the same things—or "everything." The more customized your messages, the more meaningful they're likely to be for each recipient.
3. **How can we reach them?** One audience may warrant a one-on-one meeting, a private dinner, or a series of phone calls. Another might best be addressed in a meeting or in a videoconference. E-mail or letters might do for a third group. The point is, different methods of communication have a different impact and are appropriate for different audiences.
4. **How should they respond?** What do you want them to *do*? If you're not sure, you're likely to be vague about both your message and your medium, so you won't have the impact you want.

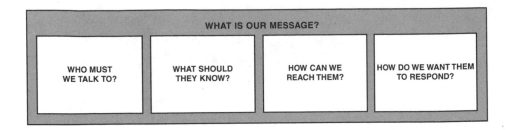

Figure 3-13 *Strategic conversation is the leader's tool for creating a winning context.*

FROM INTENTIONS TO ACTION IN 30 DAYS

Worldwide, about three out of four change programs—productivity improvement, cost reduction, customer service, a shift in strategy, or whatever—do not deliver the results that managers expect. There are many reasons for this dismal record. One is the fact that managers assume that "change takes time," and they allow too much time for it to happen. Result: there's no urgency and the wheels spin. People stay busy with "real work" while new initiatives are pushed to one side.

A second reason is that the very executives who champion new initiatives, making fine speeches about them and committing fortunes to them, are the ones who lose interest fastest. When they move on to other things, so do their people. In the process, the executives show that they were never serious in the first place, which ensures they'll never be taken seriously again.

The best way to deal with both these realities is simply to set tighter dead lines, to induce real "heat" into the system, and to move forward aggressively in small, measurable steps—and, above all, to lead visibly, to walk your talk, and to stay "on message."

> **Achievement is the best teacher. When you do, you learn. What's more, since things change so fast around a company, it makes sense to stay in constant motion, to experiment, learn, and adapt rapidly.**

Most executives are horrified at the idea of 30-day planning cycles. "That's not *strategy*," they say, "it's *tactics*." But the label doesn't matter. What does matter is that you produce results. And this is the surest way to do it.

So here's how:

1. **Every 30 days, sit down with your team, and, referring to your strategy wheel, decide on the few most important actions you should take.** Forget about trying to include everything; list just the most important things. You should end up with a handful of items under each heading on the wheel.

2. **Make someone responsible for each action.** Add names and dates. Some actions will take longer than 30 days, but the question is, what can you do within that time to get things moving? Some things will be finished sooner— maybe even in a day or two.

3. **In 30 days' time, get together again and check your progress.** Start by asking: what's changed? This will ensure that you're not surprised and that you can build your next 30-day plan to take account of the new realities. Then drill down into your lists and record how you've fared and where you have fallen behind.

Reviews need to be tough (but respectful), and participants must know that they cannot come unprepared and get away with excuses and that if they haven't delivered, they're in trouble. In no time at all, they'll get into the habit of thinking carefully about what's happening around them, of being sensible about what they commit to doing—and of actually doing it.

But a word of warning: when people realize that you're not fooling around, they are likely to stop stretching themselves and commit only to what they're 100 percent sure they can do. Don't let them get away with it! As their leader, you have to balance possibilities and realities. While it's demotivating to set impossible goals, it's worse to keep lowering your sights. So keep pushing. Keep reminding your people of your purpose and your larger goals, and insist on bold action. Most will rise to the challenge.

Strategy is about process. So is leadership. By crafting your strategic conversation the way I've suggested, you'll engage your people in a healthy growth experience. Their involvement will change their minds—and, we hope, *yours*, too. But the real transformation will come about in the follow-through, in what you push them to do.

Strategy without strong leadership is nothing. Many attempts at participative management have failed because so-called leaders gave away their responsibility and put more effort into making people happy than into inspiring them to perform. Trying to show that "people are our most important asset," they set themselves up for failure.

Strategic conversation must be both robust and respectful. It must create space not just for polite disagreement but also for heated exchanges and a serious testing of assumptions, opinions, and ideas. The leader's responsibility is to keep the conversation focused, to manage the tensions, and to keep all eyes on the future.

Since the buck stops on the leader's desk, he or she finally calls the shots. Everyone must understand this. They're most likely to accept it when they have shared in the "big conversation," have had a fair chance to speak their minds, and are themselves on the line for results.

Strategic conversation is the ultimate source of competitive advantage. But it's the way you use this tool that makes the difference.

CONCLUSION

So there it is. Everything you need to know about creating and implementing a radical strategy or clarifying your current strategy and driving it forward. All the theory is wrapped up in one neat package, a simple yet practical approach to help you make sense of complexity, cut through the b.s., and get quickly to the real point.

To summarize:

- Over time, companies have to adapt to their environment. Some of what works today will work for some time into the future; some things need to be abandoned fast. The challenge is to decide what to keep doing and what to change.
- Growth is both necessary and good. It depends more on what happens *inside* an organization than on what happens outside.
- Organizations are "open systems": information travels in and out of them, and within them. The more open a company, the more likely it is to survive in a constantly evolving, chaotic world. When you block the information flow, it becomes impossible to see either problems or opportunities or to respond to them fast and well.
- As a strategist, you have three basic tasks: (1) to choose where to focus and how to move faster along the value and cost paths than your competitors, (2) to persuade a critical mass of key people to support you so that it actually happens, and (3) to build capacity for the future.
- Your two most valuable competitive weapons are the imagination and spirit of your people.
- If there's one management saying that has been overused, it is "What gets measured gets managed." It may be true, but what everyone conveniently forgets is that it's only what gets *talked* about that will be either measured or

managed. Even the most exciting priorities have a way of dropping off the radar screen when they're not repeated, discussed, emphasized, and celebrated at every possible opportunity.

- Business is about relationships. It's a conversation between stakeholders. So organizations are "managed conversations."
- Strategic conversation is the ultimate source of competitive advantage and the most powerful business tool of all. Yet it's ignored and misused. Given that it gets so little time and attention, and that few executives use it either deliberately or well, it's little wonder that so many clever strategies deliver less than expected.
- Conversation is a two-way exchange that involves both speaking and listening. Yet many executives are not only unclear when they speak; they are also very bad listeners. And they go out of their way to shut out information, opinions, and ideas that might change the way they do things.
- Managing the "strategic conversation" is the pivotal leadership task. It's the most critical thing any executive can do. But it's more than making speeches or spelling out goals. Rather, it's a process of give and take, of hearing, caring, sharing, and growing together—a truly democratic activity, but one that must be shaped and driven—and, yes, *controlled*—with a specific purpose.
- Your strategic conversation cannot be left to chance. Far better that you think about it carefully, craft it to meet your exact needs, and use it constantly and consistently.
- If executives spent more time honing their messages and put more effort into communicating them, they would greatly improve their effectiveness. Instead, they skip this task or treat it carelessly, then struggle to fix the problems that breed in the vacuum they create.
- Strategy is usually a task reserved for a few people at the top of an organization. The output is usually a document so thick and turgid no one will ever look at it, let alone be turned on by it. And, in any event, things change so fast that whatever is written is obsolete before the ink is dry.

- If you intend to inspire a business revolution, you need to involve people in "big conversation." That means you need to spend time in the trenches, not in an ivory tower. You need to be with the people who'll make extraordinary things happen, not those who just talk about what could happen. (I hope, this book will set you free to do just that.)
- Strategy is change management. Thinking and acting are tightly intertwined activities. To separate them is to court trouble.
- To assume that "change takes time" is the kiss of death. For one thing, you don't have time. Second, when you give people time, the wheels spin. While you're waiting, nothing happens. So cut your deadlines and get moving!
- Strategy is a questioning process. It is essential that you are open and honest in dealing with the critical questions and that you foster a robust yet respectful conversation about your options.
- Your business logic must make sense. If it doesn't add up, you won't sell it to anyone—and your organization won't survive for long.
- The future will see a race to create innovative business models. Delivering superior value to customers requires the reinvention of everything you do and the way you do everything.
- Forget about changing your organization's culture. Focus on action, instead. That will change "the way we do things around here" faster than anything.
- Twenty questions and 30-day strategies—that's the way to get to the future first.

But maybe you think it can't be this easy. Perhaps you want more "meat." The bibliography on page 91 will keep you busy. But I've been there, so here's a word of advice: you really don't need to bother!

Management writers have all been saying roughly the same things for a long time. They've invented the same old wheel over and over again. They have been remarkably uncreative, and they seldom admit to their limitations.

A lot of what you hear or read about management is just puffery. It hasn't worked for others, and it won't work for you—and the proof is everywhere.

(What happened, for example, to T-groups . . . reengineering . . . scenarios . . . "generic strategies"? And consider the huge number of recent books on how to win at e-commerce!) But there are a few things that every organization must do, and you ignore them at your peril.

Managers seem to think that if things are complicated, they have some special value. They've gone crazy in their quest for easy answers, mostly by devouring complex theories.

But there aren't any silver bullets in business. There are just hard questions. Hard decisions. Hard work. And the 26 letters in the alphabet are all you have to work with.

THE 20 STRATEGY QUESTIONS

1. **Why do we exist—i.e., what is our** PURPOSE?
   - 1.1. Whom do we serve?
   - 1.2. What value do we deliver?
   - 1.3. Why do we matter?
   - 1.4. What is our ambition?

2. **How do we make money—i.e., what is our** BUSINESS RECIPE?
   - 2.1. What is our "difference"?
   - 2.2. How do we deliver our value proposition?
   - 2.3. What makes our strategy superior?
   - 2.4. How will it evolve?

3. **What kind of organization should we be—i.e., what should our** ORGANIZATIONAL CHARACTER **be?**
   - 3.1. What assumptions guide us?
   - 3.2. What turns us on?
   - 3.3. What is not negotiable?
   - 3.4. How do we behave?

4. **What must we do, and how will we make it happen—i.e., what are our** GOALS **and** PRIORITIES, **and what** ACTIONS **must we take?**
   - 4.1. What results do we seek? (Goals)
   - 4.2. On what few *high-impact* issues must we concentrate our resources? (Priorities)
   - 4.3. What must we do about them—i.e., what action must we take?
   - 4.4. What must we do *in the next 30 days*, and who is responsible?

5. **How will we win the support of our stakeholders—i.e., what STRATEGIC CONVERSATION will capture their attention and imagination, and how will we reach them?**
   5.1. Whom must we talk to?
   5.2. What do they need to know?
   5.3. How can we reach them?
   5.4. How should they respond?

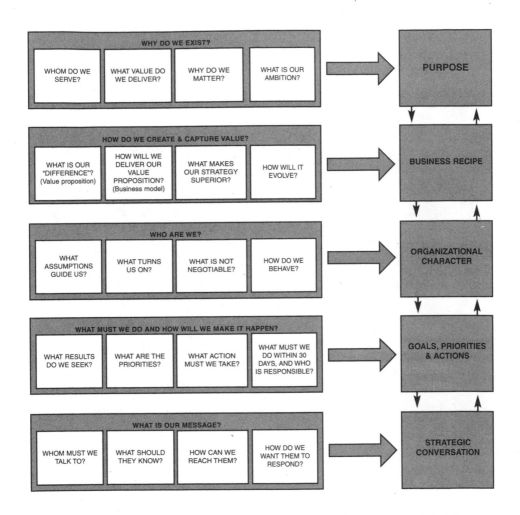

Figure 4-1 *These 20 questions embrace vital issues and ensure that you think through your strategy in a methodical way. But, equally important, they add up to a strategic conversation that will let you make a difference. Use them to analyze your current situation and to explore future possibilities.*

NOTES

1. For a fascinating history of futurists' failures, see William A. Sherden, *The Fortune Sellers* (New York: Wiley, 1999). For amusing quotes on the future, see Christopher Cerf and Victor Nasavsky, *The Experts Speak* (New York: Pantheon Books, 1984).

2. My 7Ps framework was inspired by a series of articles in the *Harvard Business Review* by Christopher Bartlett and Sumantra Goshal—"Beyond Strategy to Purpose" (November–December 1994), "Beyond Structure to Processes" (January–February 1995), and "Beyond Systems to People" (May–June 1995)—which later formed the basis of their wonderful book, *The Individualized Organization* (New York: HarperBusiness, 1997). But whereas they focused on purpose, processes, and people, I have added four other elements—philosophies, products, positioning, and partners—that are critical to a company's design. A questionnaire to help you work through my framework is available on my website at www.tonymanning.com.

3. As Michael Porter points out in his article "What Is Strategy?" (*Harvard Business Review*, November–December 1996), a competitor might be able to copy one part of your "activity system," but the chances of copying two are less good, and, as you continue to add differences, the odds shrink fast: $.9 \times .9 = .81$; $.9 \times .9 \times .9 \times .9 = .66$; and so on.

RECOMMENDED READING

Michael Beer and Nitin Nohria, *Breaking The Code of Change*, Boston: Harvard Business School Press, 2000.

John Seely Brown and Paul Duguid, *The Social Life of Information*, Boston: Harvard Business School Press, 2000.

Shona L. Brown and Kathleen M. Eisenhardt, *Competing on the Edge*, Boston: Harvard Business School Press, 1998.

Ritha Gunther McGrath and Ian MacMillan, *The Entrepreneurial Mindset*, Boston: Harvard Business School Press, 2000.

William Isaacs, *Dialogue*, New York: Currency Doubleday, 2000.

John Kao, *Jamming*, New York: HarperBusiness, 1996.

Henry Mintzberg, Bruce Ahlstrand, and Joseph Lamel, *Strategy Safari*, New York: Free Press, 1998.

Richard Normann and Rafael Ramirez, *Designing Interactive Strategy*, New York: Wiley, 1994, 1998.

Charles O'Reilly III and Jeffrey Pfeffer, *Hidden Value*, Boston: Harvard Business School Press, 2000.

Paul Ormerod, *Butterfly Economics*, New York: Pantheon Books, 1998.

James O'Toole, *Leading Change*, San Francisco: Jossey-Bass, 1995.

Richard Pascale, Mark Millemann, and Linda Gioja, *Surfing The Edge of Chaos*, New York: Crown Business, 2000.

Jeffrey Pfeffer and Robert I. Sutton, *The Knowing-Doing Gap*, Boston: Harvard Business School Press, 2000.

Virginia Postrel, *The Future and Its Enemies*, New York: Free Press, 1998.

Michael Schrage, *Serious Play*, Boston: Harvard Business School Press, 2000.

Howard Sherman and Ron Schultz, *Open Boundaries*, New York: Perseus Books, 1998.

Michael J. Silverstein and George Stalk, Jr., eds., *Breaking Compromises*, New York: Wiley, 2000.

Georg Von Krogh, Kazuo Ichijo, and Ikujiro Nonaka, *Enabling Knowledge Creation*, New York: Oxford University Press, 2000.

INDEX

acting to learn, 41
action plan, 71–76
Alcoholics Anonymous, 43
anticipation, 14
assumptions
    danger of glib, 51
    identifying, 70
    strategic, 49–50, 57

balanced scorecard, 71
behavior(s)
    changing, 43
    identifying, 70
"big conversations," 46, 47,
    79
"big issues, the," 9
brands, 25
"breakthrough" products,
    24
business cycles, 56–57
business design, 27
business execution, 14, 27,
    40, 71
business logic, 54–57
business model(s)

designing your, 53, 66–70
new, 24
and strategic process,
    66–70
business purpose, 63–64, 68
business recipe, definition
    of, 65–66

capabilities, 11
capacity, building, 7
change, 14
change cycle, 41–42
change management,
    40–42
character, organizational,
    70–71
climate, 36, 44–45
command-and-control
    approach, 63
commitment, 28
competition, 19, 26–27
    and business arena, 58,
        60–61
    and business model, 66
competitiveness, 37

ABOUT THE AUTHOR

Tony Manning has been an independent consultant since 1987, specializing in change management, competitive strategy, and corporate turnarounds. He was previously the Chairman and CEO of McCann-Erickson in South Africa and a senior marketing executive with Coca-Cola. Elected Chairman of the Institute of Directors of Southern Africa in 1999, he is the author of six previous management books. Mr. Manning hails from Morningside, South Africa.

DATE DUE

2/28/13	

DEMCO, INC. 38-2931

Survival and success depend on *innovation*. So strategy has to be about:

1. Being alert to change (ANTICIPATION).
2. Seeing opportunities to offer something different and new (INSIGHT).
3. Dreaming up new ways of doing it (IMAGINATION).
4. Doing it consistently and to the highest standards (EXECUTION).

The question, of course, is *when* and *what* do you change? (*How* comes later.) These are always risk decisions. Much of what your company does today might have great value for a long time yet. To drop some of your products now could be ill advised. To add bells and whistles to your services might add costs but bring no immediate benefits. To reengineer your processes might cause more problems than it's worth. To change your advertising campaign might be a sure way to destroy your brand in the marketplace.

Change for the sake of change is stupid. There has to be a business case for it. But when the case is clear, don't resist or even *hesitate*. (It's insane to do more of the same while expecting different results!) However strong your inclination may be to hold your course, there comes a time when you have to act. Often a window of opportunity opens for only a brief moment. Seize that moment, and you gain advantage; miss it, and you may never recover.

For some businesses, the smartest thing to do is to strive constantly and aggressively for disruptive strategies—to change not just the rules of their game but the game itself. In other cases, the best way forward is to stay with the basics, to hone them continuously, to execute meticulously, and to make substantial changes rarely.

As a general principle, every company should aim for both improvement *and* radical change. This is hard to do, but it's also hard for competitors to match. When you present a constantly moving target, they're pressed to keep up with you. And the *more things* you change, and the *faster* you do it, the better your chances of staying out front. In a street fight, a surgical strike may save your life but a "flurry of blows" keeps your enemy off balance and sets you up for the big hit.